ONLY FOOLS
★ and ★
HORSES
QUIZ BOOK

ONLY FOOLS
★ and ★
HORSES
QUIZ BOOK

**He Who Dares Quizzes:
Over 1,000 Questions on
The Greatest Show Ever**

JOHN WHITE

JOHN BLAKE

First published in the UK by John Blake Publishing
An imprint of Bonnier Books UK
80–1 Wimpole Street, London, W1G 9RE
Owned by Bonnier Books
Sveavägen 56, Stockholm, Sweden

facebook.com/johnblakebooks ❶
twitter.com/jblakebooks ❏

First published in paperback in 2009
This edition published in 2020

Hardback – 978-1-78946-393-4
Ebook – 978-1-78946-442-9

A CIP catalogue of this book is available from the British Library.

Design by www.envydesign.co.uk
Illustrations by Frankie Dodds

Printed and bound by Clays Ltd, Elcograf S.p.A

3 5 7 9 10 8 6 4

Copyright © John White, 2009

John White has asserted his moral right to be identified as the author of this
Work in accordance with the Copyright, Designs and Patents Act 1988.

John Blake Publishing is an imprint of Bonnier Books UK
www.bonnierbooks.co.uk

I am dedicating this book to all the fans of the show and in particular to Janice, our two sons, Marc and Paul, and last but certainly not least to my father-in-law, Robert 'Bobby' McWilliams, who sadly left us on 22 May, 2008. Bobby was a massive fan of the show and constantly borrowed my video tapes and DVDs of *Only Fools and Horses* to sit for hours on end at home in his armchair chuckling at the hilarious exploits of Del Boy & Co.

Fabrique Belgique Mon Ami

Danka

Chambourcie Nouvel

Luvly Jubbly

INTRODUCTION

From the very first moment that *Only Fools and Horses* burst on to our TV screens in September 1981, I have been hooked. I will never forget the very first Episode, 'Big Brother', which brought Del Boy, Grandad and Rodney (the Trotters), into my life. I say 'my life' because I have been a fan of the show ever since.

Like many of you I have my own favourite episodes and my own favourite moments from the show. Just thinking about Del Boy and Rodney standing beneath one of the chandeliers in 'A Touch of Glass' and then watching Grandad nonchalantly walking down the stairs after the matching chandelier crashed to the ground, still has me in fits of laughter. Or who will ever forget the scene from 'Danger UXD' when the erotic blow-up dolls suddenly self-inflated at the Trotters' flat. Absolutely classic moments and part of the reason why *Only Fools and Horses* was voted best British comedy of all time a few years ago. And so to John Sullivan, the creator and writer of *Only Fools and Horses*: just how this man managed to keep us laughing with all the comings and goings at Trotters Independent Traders over the 20+ years the Trotters were beamed into our living rooms is a testament to his writing genius. Thank you so much Mr Sullivan for so many fond memories and countless laughs along the way.

And by way of special thanks, I would like to thank my mate JD for helping me with proofreading my text and Frankie ('Dodger') for contributing all of the wonderful sketches throughout my quiz book. But most of all I want to thank my wife, Janice, for all her hard work in helping me develop my idea into the finished product.

Bonjour!

John White

CONTENTS

CONTENTS

CONTENTS

CONTENTS

CHRISTMAS SPECIALS

RE-ARRANGE THE EPISODE TITLES TO MATCH THE YEAR THE CHRISTMAS SPECIALS WERE SHOWN

1	'The Jolly Boys Outing'	1991

2	'Diamonds are for Heather'	1987

3	'A Royal Flush'	1990

4	'Mother Nature's Son'	1989

5 .	'Christmas Crackers'	1985

FIND THE
EPISODE

RE-ARRANGE THE EPISODE TITLES BASED ON THE CLUE GIVEN

15 ROT FEAT HERE [A Cosy Meal]

....

16 WED TAN [In Demand]

....

17 SOUND THE ROME ATE CIND [Del's Been Down This Road Before]

....

18 FOR THEY THOU WAY MICE BE [Sounds like A Line From Star Wars]

....

19 HE ATE HER MAD FONDS RAIRO [This Girl's Best Friend?]

....

20 SWAG FELLO THE THONGEL [Tall Policewoman]

....

21 A CLAG SHOUTS OF [Broken Pieces]

....

22 THE WELLY ROPE LI [Sunglasses Needed For Kitchen]

....

23 IAN IN KISS THE CLAWS END [Unwell And Rich]

....

24 THE FIGG STAR [Nervous Jitters]

....

MATCH THE EPISODE WITH THE SERIES

LISTED BELOW ARE THE NAMES OF SEVEN EPISODES. CAN YOU MATCH THE EPISODE WITH THE SERIES IT BELONGS TO?

25	'Danger UXD'	Series 4
26	'Ashes to Ashes'	Series 3
27	'Cash and Curry'	Series 6
28	'The Class of '62'	Series 2
29	'Hole in One'	Series 7
30	'Friday The 14th'	Series 5
31	'The Miracle of Peckham'	Series 1

Series 1 ....

Series 2 ....

Series 3 ....

Series 4 ....

Series 5 ....

Series 6 ....

Series 7 ....

DEL BOY – 1

32   What is the real name of the actor who plays Del Boy: David Jason, David Trotter or David White?

....

33   What actor's role in the sitcom *Dad's Army* was offered to David, only for it to be later taken away from him?

....

34   In which city was David born?

....

35   What was the name of the BBC series in which David starred alongside Ronnie Barker as a delivery boy/shop assistant?

....

36　What was the name of David's character in the series in No. 35?

....

37　Can you name the children's comedy series in which David got his first television break?

....

38　What was David's first job after he left school aged 15?

....

39　True or False, David once had a part in the series *Crossroads*?

....

40　Can you name the character David played in *Porridge*?

....

41　True or False, David's first starring role was in a series named *Hark at Barker*?

....

RODNEY – 1

42   What is Rodney's real name?

....

43   Can you recall the name of the BBC series in which he starred
alongside Wendy Craig?

....

44   What was the name of his character in the above series: Adam,
Martin or Stephen?

....

45   True or False, he starred in the BBC series, *The Prince and
the Pauper*?

....

46 How many GCE (GCSE) 'O' Levels did Rodney Trotter pass at school?

....

47 In what subject(s) did Rodney Trotter obtain an 'O' Level?

....

48 In which episode did Rodney fall in love with a policewoman?

....

49 True or False, he starred in *Porridge*?

....

50 What is Rodney Trotter's middle name?

....

51 What final position on the local housing committee did Rodney get landed with in the episode 'Homesick'?

....

I KNOW WHAT IT'S CALLED

CAN YOU NAME THE EPISODE FROM THE CLUES GIVEN BELOW?

52 Del and Rodney's father turns up one Christmas at the flat. The boys' Dad claims to be seriously ill and persuades the boys to have their blood tested. Their Dad alters Del Boy's blood group, casting doubt that Del and Rodney both had the same father. Rodney and Grandad get on great with the new Trotter while Del Boy remains at a distance. The truth is discovered in the end and Del Boy sends his Dad packing.

....

53 One of Del's old fiancées, Pauline, turns up at The Nag's Head. Del is smitten and falls in love with her all over again. When Del moves Pauline into the flat, Rodney and Grandad are not too pleased and decide it is time for them to leave. When Del discovers that Pauline has been widowed twice already, he decides to jump

ship as well. The boys turn up at a house they believe to be their aunt's only to discover that she had left many years before. At the end of the episode Grandad has a chat with the speaking clock in America.

....

54   A trip to the Starlight Rooms sees Del expanding his business interests and he agrees to supply a cabaret act. Del persuades Racquel to team up with one of Trigger's old workmates, Tony Angelino, only to discover that Tony cannot sing any songs with 'R's in them. Del Boy does a runner and leaves Rodney and Racquel to face the music.

....

55   Del Boy just cannot win a game of cards and seems to have no luck at all. Then he decides to organise a poker night at the flat. Boycie turns up with a briefcase full of readies and a dodgy deck or two. In the final hand Boycie thinks he has taken Del to the cleaners, believing he has won the entire contents of the flat and Trigger's car by producing four Kings. However, Del Boy has something else up his sleeve and produces a poker of Aces to win the game.

....

56   In this episode, Del Boy agrees to purchase 250 eighteen-carat gold chains from a retired jeweller. The chains aren't exactly kosher, having avoided the clutches of HM Customs & Excise. Del puts a consortium together comprising Uncle Albert, Rodney, Boycie, Trigger and Mike to purchase the chains, only to witness

their former owner suffer an apparent heart attack in a restaurant. However, all is not lost as Del gets his money back after the jeweller attempts a similar con on Denzil.

....

57   A stranger approaches Mike and books a room at The Nag's Head for a reunion with all of his classmates from 1962. Del, Boycie, Trigger and Denzil are all invited and turn up, along with Rodney, only to discover that the evening was organised by the despised Roy Slater. However, Slater has just recently been released from prison and the boys give him a second chance. A good night's drinking is had by all only for it to end with Del discovering that Slater is Racquel's husband.

....

58   Del purchases a consignment of briefcases from Trigger only to discover that no one can actually open them because the combination to each one is locked inside the case! Grandad tells the boys about the time he was a night watchman at a leather factory, and how he unwittingly allowed an employee to steal a few hundred briefcases by taking one home with him almost every night for nearly a year. This was also the first episode ever made and put the Trotters on their way to screen success.

....

59   The boys are a bit strapped for cash until Uncle Albert falls down a hole. The hole in question is the cellar door of The Nag's Head and Uncle Albert lands on Mike, the landlord. The brewery offer an out-of-court settlement but Del wants more and instructs a solicitor to

take the matter to court. Of course the boys lose their case after it is discovered that Uncle Albert had a history of falling down holes!

....

60 Del Boy purchases a consignment of paint from Trigger and persuades the local Chinese restaurant to have their kitchen painted. The only trouble is that after the paint dries it is luminous and the kitchen staff has to wear sunglasses. Del discovers that the paint is used to paint signals in railway tunnels. To make matters worse, Del Boy paints his mum's statue with the paint and now it lights up the entire graveyard.

....

WHO PLAYED WHO?

CAN YOU MATCH THE CHARACTER WITH THEIR REAL NAME?

CHARACTER

61	*Marlene*	Jamie Smith	....
62	*Sid* (Sid's Café)	Buster Merryfield	....
63	*Grandad*	John Challis	....
64	*Denzil*	Roger Lloyd Pack	....
65	*Mike*	Steven Woodcock	....
66	*Damien*	Gwyneth Strong	....
67	*Uncle Albert*	Denis Lill	....

68	*Trigger*	Sue Holderness	....
69	*Mickey*	Paul Barber	....
70	*Racquel*	Kenneth MacDonald	....
71	*Jevon*	Lennard Pearce	....
72	*Alan Parry*	Patrick Murray	....
73	*Boycie*	Tessa Peake-Jones	....
74	*Cassandra*	Roy Heather	....

MIXED BAG – 1

75 Who wrote the *Only Fools and Horses* series?

....

76 What was the name of the book written by Steve Clark as a celebration of the legendary comedy series?

....

77 A very famous actor, who possesses a knighthood, and who is a huge fan of the show, wrote the foreword to the book in No. 76. Can you name him?

....

78 What was the name of the very first episode?

....

79 In what year was No. 78 first shown?

....

80　What tool did the madman in the episode 'Friday The 14th' use
on his victims?

....

81　Beginning with 'J', what was the name of the barmaid in No. 78?

....

82　Whose grandfather's ashes did Del try to dispose of in the episode
'Ashes to Ashes'?

....

83　What were the ashes in No. 82 kept in?

....

84　True or False, John Sullivan both wrote and sang the theme song
to the series?

....

CAN YOU GUESS THE EPISODE FROM THE NAME OF A SONG THAT WAS HEARD IN IT AND A CLUE TOWARDS ITS IDENTITY?

	SONG	CLUE
85	'High Fly'	A dead budgie is found in the kitchen of Denzil's flat
86	'Lady in Red'	Rodney thought he was chatting up a Swedish girl who turned out to be German and pregnant
87	'Love Goes Up And Down'	Rodney meets Cassandra for the first time and Del Boy falls down in the yuppy bistro

88	'Ain't No Stopping Us Now'	Del Boy decides to become a second-hand car salesman, which backfires on him when the car he sold smashes into Boycie's sports car
89	'Rockin' All Over The World'	Barry Gibb wasn't too happy when Del Boy spotted him in the garden of his luxury home
90	'Delilah'	Tony Angelino gave his best Tom Jones' impersonation
91	'2,4,6,8'	The boys head off to the seaside for the day and their coach catches fire at a pub en-route
92	'Birdie Song'	A painting by a young Rodney wins a holiday for three but his joy is short-lived when he discovers Cassandra has to pretend to be his step mum
93	'West End Girls'	Rodney is commissioned to make a film while Del makes a financial killing signing up all the locals to star in it.

94 'Money'   Del is conned into paying £2,000
for what he thinks is a priceless
Indian relic. Sounds like he visited
the wholesalers!

....

95   How many episodes were there in Series 1: five, seven or nine?

....

96   The last episode in Series 1 has the same title as something you would find on most dinner tables at Christmas, and which you must pull. Can you name the episode?

....

97   Who appeared in Series 1 first, Boycie or Trigger?

....

98   What type of car did Boycie ask Del Boy to look after for him in 'Go West Young Man'?

....

99 What did Del Boy discover under a pile of bricks he purchased
    in 'The Russians are Coming'?

....

100 Complete the title: 'A Slow Bus To ....'

....

101 How many legs did Del Boy claim the turkeys he was selling
     in 'Big Brother' have?

....

102 What was the name of Del Boy's former girlfriend who turned
     up in 'The Second Time Around'?

....

103 What did the policeman in 'The Russians are Coming' ask
     Del Boy to look out for?

....

104 In Episode 5 of Series 1 (*see* No. 100), Del Boy started up a
     coach/travel company. Can you recall the name of the
     coach/travel company?

....

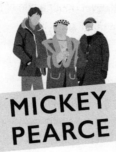

MICKEY PEARCE

105 'Mickey' was played by Patrick Murray. Can you name the ITV cop show Patrick has also starred in?

....

106 In what episode did the Driscoll Brothers break Mickey's arm?

....

107 What items of electronic equipment did Mickey and his pal purchase in No. 106?

....

108 True or False, Mickey was spotted by the producer of *Only Fools and Horses* in a McDonald's advertisement?

....

109 In what series did Mickey join the show: 1, 2 or 3?

....

110 Can you name the first episode he starred in? In it, Rodney
decided to end his partnership with Del and both he and Mickey
went into business.

....

111 What did Rodney and Mickey purchase at an auction that led
Mickey to suggest they sell the items to some 'carrot crunchers'?

....

112 What was Mickey's most distinct item of clothing?

....

113 In the episode 'Watching the Girls Go By', Rodney and Mickey
agree a bet. How much was their bet for?

....

114 When he was young Patrick played a starring role in a film about
life in a boy's borstal. Do you know what the film is called?

....

'BIG BROTHER'

115 This was the first episode to hit our TV screens, but who did we see first: Del Boy, Rodney or Grandad?

....

116 What did Del Boy purchase from Trigger?

....

117 How much did he pay for the items in No. 116?

....

118 Why was Grandad so upset with Rodney?

....

119 Can you name the cartoon character that was on Rodney's T-shirt?

....

120 Grandad mentioned Del Boy's father predicting that a football team would win the Cup. Can you name the team?

....

121 In the episode, Rodney decided to go abroad. Where did he tell Grandad he was going?

....

122 When Rodney eventually returned home, where in France did he inform Del Boy he managed to go as far as?

....

123 How far did Rodney actually get?

....

124 Why was he not able to reach his target destination in No. 121?

....

MIXED BAG - 2

125 What was the name of the episode that introduced Boycie?

....

126 Who produced the show from 1981 to 1987?

....

127 In the show, what was the name of the block of flats the Trotters lived in?

....

128 What make of vehicle (van) did the Trotters use for their business?

....

129 What three cities/towns are written on the side of the van?

....

130 True or False, Grandad smoked?

....

131 What were the first words of French uttered by Del Boy in an episode?

....

132 How many years separated Del Boy and Rodney: 13, 15 or 17?

....

133 What was the first car Del Boy purchased when he decided to become a second-hand car salesman?

....

134 How old was Rodney when his mum died: six, eight or ten?

....

HOOKY GEAR

ALL YOU HAVE TO DO HERE IS MATCH THE 'HOOKY GEAR' WITH THE EPISODE DEL BOY TRIED TO FLOG THEM IN

135 Women's Clothing   'A Slow Bus to Chingford'

....

136 Louvre Doors   'The Miracle of Peckham'

....

137 Second-hand Cars   'Danger UXD'

....

138 Lawn Mower Engines   'Big Brother'

....

139	Paint	'As One Door Closes'
140	Lead	'No Greater Love'
141	A Baby	'Healthy Competition'
142	Briefcases	'Go West Young Man'
143	Ethnic Tours	'The Yellow Peril'
144	Blow-Up Dolls	'From Prussia With Love'

MIXED BAG – 3

145 What country did the Trotters visit in 'It Never Rains…'?

....

146 In 'Friday The 14th', who did the axe murderer kill?

....

147 Complete the title, 'Diamonds Are For ………'

....

148 In 'Big Brother', what type of fuel did Del Boy use to describe Grandad's former occupation?

....

149 What was the name of Boycie and Marlene's son?

....

150 Apart from Only Fools and Horses, can you name the series, starring David Jason that Gwyneth Strong (Cassandra) also appeared in?

....

151 True or False, Paul Barber (Denzil) also played a role in Brookside?

....

152 Kenneth MacDonald (Mike) played a part in a series that portrayed actor, Jimmy Nail, as a singer. Name the snappy series.

....

153 In the episode, 'Sickness and Wealth we discovered Boycie's real Christian name. Can you remember what it is?

....

154 In the episode 'Dates', what did Trigger give as his occupation to the dating agency?

....

SLATER

155 What was the title of the first episode we saw Slater in?

....

156 Can you recall his first name?

....

157 How did he manage to get into the Trotter's flat in No. 155?

....

158 What stolen item was he looking for in No. 155?

....

159 True or False, he used to be married to Boycie's wife?

....

160 What episode did he get arrested in?

....

161 What was he attempting to steal in No. 160?

....

162 Can you recall the surname of his driver in No. 160?

....

163 In what episode did he organise a get together in?

....

164 After being released from jail, what job did he get?

....

'GO WEST YOUNG MAN'

165 Rodney was having girlfriend problems in this episode.
What was the name of his girlfriend: Stacey, Janice or Monica?

....

166 One of Rodney's mates suggested that Rodney should take a trial
separation from the girl in No. 165. Who was the mate in question
and how many weeks did he suggest for the trial?

....

167 Del Boy decided to try his hand at the second-hand car market
and purchased a car from Boycie. What make of vehicle did
he buy?

....

168 Del Boy paid £25 for the car in No. 167 but how much did he
sell it for: £99, £199 or £299?

....

169 When Boycie asked Del to look after an E-type Jaguar for him, Boycie mentioned that it was only Jaguars and a certain British athlete that made him proud to be British. Can you recall the name of the athlete?

....

170 When Del Boy purchased the car in No. 167 there were 88,000 miles on the clock. How many miles were on the clock when he sold it: 23,000, 33,000 or 43,000?

....

171 What did Del Boy put in the glove compartment of the car and then claim that it had been left there by the previous owner?

....

172 What horse-sounding name did Del Boy give to the cocktail that he ordered in the gay bar?

....

173 Del Boy claimed that Roger Moore had one of the cocktails (*in* No. 172) in *Live And Let Die*. When Rodney ordered half a lager what was the waiter's response?

....

174 On what did Del Boy write the telephone numbers of the two girls that both he and Rodney chatted up in a nightclub, and what did Rodney do with the item?

....

DEL BOY'S FOREIGN LINGO

IN SOME OF THE FOLLOWING QUESTIONS YOU ARE REQUIRED TO COMPLETE DEL BOY'S 'FOREIGN' PHRASE

175 '*Chambourcie* ....'

....

176 What French word(s) does Del Boy use to say '*Hello*'?

....

177 '*Vorsprung Dork* ....'

....

178 '............... *Belgique*'

....

179 What word beginning with the letter 'I' does Del use the term
     '*Pranny*' for?

     ....

180 '*Plume De Ma* ....'

     ....

181 Can you name Argentinean-born Real Madrid centre forward
     from the 1960s whose surname was used by Del Boy when
     something gave him great pleasure?

     ....

182 What French word does Del Boy use to say '*Goodbye*'?

     ....

183 Del Boy is often heard screaming, '*You* ...., *Rodney.*'

     ....

184 When Del Boy described the quality of the diamonds in
     'To Hull and Back', what word, beginning with the letter 'P',
     did he use?

     ....

DENZIL

185 Where in England was Paul Barber, who played Denzil, born?

....

186 What was the name of the TV show that Paul starred in alongside a character named *Yosser Hughes*?

....

187 What occupation did Denzil have in 'To Hull and Back'?

....

188 What episode involving a budgie did Denzil first appear in?

....

189 Can you recall the name of Denzil's wife?

....

DENZIL

190 Del Boy agreed to do the catering for Denzil's wedding. What type of cake did he end up supplying for the bride and groom?

....

191 What was the name of the episode in which Del Boy persuaded Denzil to sign over a consignment of faulty dolls to him?

....

192 Paul co-starred in a film alongside Robert Carlyle that was a smash hit in the late 1990s. Can you name the film?

....

193 What was the nickname of Paul's character in the film referred to in No. 192?

....

194 True or False, Denzil lived in Nelson Mandela House?

....

'CASH AND CURRY'

195 What make of car did Del Boy drive in 'Cash and Curry'?

....

196 This episode was about two Indians who pretended they did not
     speak to one another. Can you recall either of their names?

....

197 One of the Indian gentlemen had a driver who held a Second Dan
     in karate. What did Del Boy say he had?

....

198 At one point Rodney burst into the restaurant to help Del Boy out.
     What item of cutlery did Rodney lift to protect himself?

....

199 The entire episode centred on a statue. Can you name the statue?

....

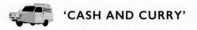

200 Which Hindu god did one of the Indian gentlemen say the statue was?

....

201 Who did Del think the name of the Hindu god was?

....

202 What Victorian item did Del Boy claim that his mum left him and Rodney as a family heirloom?

....

203 Del Boy likened a situation in the episode to the '*chicken and egg*' story but what did Del Boy replace the word '*chicken*' with?

....

204 To raise money to purchase the statue Del Boy pawned all of his jewellery. How many gold carats did he claim to Rodney that it added up to?

....

NO.1 HITS - 1

ALL YOU HAVE TO DO HERE IS MATCH THE SONG THAT WAS NO. I IN THE BRITISH RECORD CHARTS WITH THE EPISODE THAT WAS FIRST TELEVISED AT THE SAME TIME

	SONG	EPISODE
205	'Do You Really Want To Hurt Me' (1982) by Culture Club	'Friday The 14th'
206	'2 Become 1' (1996) by The Spice Girls	'To Hull and Back'
207	'Caravan Of Love' (1986) by The Housemartins	'Ashes to Ashes'

208 'Tainted Love'   'Sickness and Wealth'
(1981) by Soft Cell

....

209 'Especially For You'   'Time On Our Hands'
(1989) by Kylie Minogue/Jason Donovan

....

210 'Uptown Girl'   'A Slow Bus to Chingford'
(1983) by Billy Joel

....

211 'Only You'   'A Royal Flush'
(1983) by The Flying Pickets

....

212 'Something's Gotten Hold Of My Heart'   'Big Brother'
(1989) by Marc Almond with Gene Pitney

....

...

213 'Prince Charming'   'Who's a Pretty Boy?'
(1981) by Adam & The Ants

....

214 'Saving All My Love For You'   'Danger UXD'
(1985) by Whitney Houston

....

MIXED BAG – 4

215 If Del Boy gave you 'a douce in bunce' how much money would you have?

....

216 In 'Go West Young Man', Del Boy dropped the keys to Boycie's Jaguar and claimed that the vehicle belonged to Rodney. What make of car did Del Boy claim to own?

....

217 In 'Cash and Curry', how much did Del Boy persuade the owner of the statue to sell it for: £2,000, £6,000 or £8,000?

....

218 In 'Diamonds Are for Heather', what did Del say was so tough that it asked him for a fight in the car park twice?

....

219 In 'Who Wants To Be A Millionaire?' what two brothers did Uncle
Albert say Del Boy and Rodney reminded him of: The Charlton
Brothers, The Driscoll Brothers or The Ewing Brothers?

....

220 Complete Del Boy's famous line, '*This time next year we'll be...*'

....

221 In 'To Hull and Back' Del Boy greeted one of the Dutchmen with
a greeting that is the name of a Dutch football team. Can you
recall what Del Boy said?

....

222 A die-cast replica model of the Trotters' three-wheel van can be
purchased in the shops. Which company produced it: Corgi, Dinky
or Lledo?

....

223 How many million viewers tuned in to watch 'Time On Our Hands',
Christmas 1996?

....

224 In addition to a watch, what item of jewellery did Del Boy wear on
his wrist in many of the episodes?

....

UNCLE ALBERT – 1

225 What is Uncle Albert's real name: Buster Cherryfield, Buster Merryfield or Buster Stoneyfield?

....

226 In which episode do we first see Uncle Albert?

....

227 Whereabouts did he fall asleep in the Trotters' flat in No. 226?

....

228 What type of overcoat did we always see him wear?

....

229 Complete his famous line '*During the.........*'

....

230 What was Buster's occupation before he turned to acting on a full-time basis?

....

231 True or False, during the war Buster became Southern Command Army Boxing Champion in 1945?

....

232 What was Uncle Albert's favourite drink?

....

233 True or False, Uncle Albert was Grandad's older brother?

....

234 What is the title of Buster's autobiography?

....

GRANDAD

235 Who played Grandad?

....

236 How many series did Grandad appear in?

....

237 In 'The Second Time Around' what did Pauline hide from him?

....

238 In what episode did Grandad dump the promotional leaflets
     Del Boy had printed?

....

239 True or False, Grandad appeared in *Coronation Street*?

....

240 In 'Christmas Crackers' where did Grandad go for the Old Folks Christmas Dinner?

....

241 What did Grandad burn black in 'Christmas Crackers'?

....

242 How many televisions would Grandad watch at the same time?

....

243 Grandad was arrested in two episodes. Name either of them.

....

244 Whose funeral did Grandad attend in 'Ashes to Ashes'?

....

'THE SECOND TIME AROUND'

245 Who told Del Boy that his ex-fiancée, Pauline Harris, was back
     in Peckham and asking about him: Boycie, Denzil or Trigger?

....

246 When Del Boy entered the pub he ordered a Pernod and
     blackcurrant for himself and a pint of what type of oil for Trigger?

....

247 When Del Boy asked Pauline where her husband was she said
     he was down the Blackshaw Road. Del Boy asked if he was in
     the flats there and Pauline said '*No, he is in the .... there*'.
     Complete the line.

....

248 What was Pauline's occupation: air-hostess, beauty therapist or fitness instructor?

....

249 What pop group did Del Boy tell Rodney teenage marriages broke up over in the 1960s because the husband did not like the band?

....

250 Del Boy said that he got upset when Ally McGraw died in the movie Love Story. Why did he say Rodney got upset watching the same movie?

....

251 Rodney called Pauline 'A ...... *digger*'. Complete the description.

....

252 Which one of his French lines did Del Boy use to describe the steak Pauline made him for his tea?

....

253 Which one of Del Boy's mates telephoned him and told him that the police were investigating the death of Pauline's husband?

....

254 Del Boy decided to join Rodney and Uncle Albert when they made the decision to leave the flat before Pauline returned home. Where were the boys headed?

....

'A SLOW BUS TO CHINGFORD'

255 What was the name of Rodney's girlfriend in the episode: Bernice, Denise or Janice?

....

256 What item of clothing did Rodney ask his girlfriend to take off, only for her to say that she couldn't because she wasn't wearing one!

....

257 Rodney claimed that Del Boy's only association with art was that he used to be the '*Cultural Advisor to the .... Shed*'. Fill in the name of the missing football team.

....

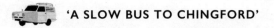

258 Why did Del Boy claim that the sculptor of the world famous Venus de Milo was 'a bit sick'?

....

259 For how much did Del Boy plan to flog the copies of the statue in No. 258?

....

260 When Del Boy woke Rodney up for work, Rodney had only had 20 minutes' sleep. Complete Del Boy's description of his brother when he said he looked like '*The son of the bride of* ....'

....

261 Del Boy formed a security company in the episode with the initials '*TW*'. What did the initials stand for?

....

262 What type of uniform did Del Boy obtain for Rodney to carry out his duties as a night watchman?

....

263 Can you recall the name, or breed, of Rodney's girlfriend's dog, which Del Boy persuaded Rodney to use as a guard dog?

....

264 In return for Rodney working as a night watchman, Del Boy was permitted the use of an open-top bus. Del Boy intended to use the bus to take tourists sightseeing in London. How much did he plan to charge for the tours: £15, £17 or £19?

....

'THE RUSSIANS ARE COMING'

265 What type of shelter did Del Boy and Rodney make from the consignment of lead they purchased?

....

266 How many minutes did Rodney say they had to get to the shelter in the event of a nuclear attack?

....

267 Where was the first place that was suggested to erect the shelter in No. 265?

....

268 During a trial run to the location in No. 267, the boys were stopped by the police for speeding. What make and model was the police car?

....

269 Can you recall the first name of either of the two police officers?

....

270 Where in Greece did the sergeant inform Del he was going for his holidays?

....

271 Whereabouts did the boys end up erecting the shelter?

....

272 Who suggested the location in No. 271: Del, Grandad or Rodney?

....

273 What type of stones did Rodney claim Del Boy had sold to the rioters during the Brixton Riots?

....

274 How many hours did each battery in the shelter last for?

....

'CHRISTMAS CRACKERS'

275   Who cooked the Trotter Family Christmas Dinner?

....

276   Grandad claimed Rodney had worms in his stomach.
      What type of worms did Del Boy say they were?

....

277   What did the person who cooked the turkey forget to take out
      of it before he cooked it?

....

278   What programme was Rodney watching on TV only to discover
      that there was a similar programme on the other side when he
      changed channels?

....

279   What colour was the Trotter's Christmas tree?

....

280   Rodney persuaded Del Boy to go out for the evening. Can you
      recall the name of the club, which sounds a bit like an F1 racing
      circuit, that the boys went to?

....

281   What film, starring Julie Andrews, was starting on TV before the
      boys decided to head out for the evening?

....

282   In the club from No. 280, what type of soda did Del Boy order
      along with his Rémy Martin?

....

283   What did Del Boy buy Rodney for Christmas: a pen, a wallet or
      a gold chain?

....

284   Del Boy wore a blue suit, red shirt and a white tie when he and
      Rodney went out for the evening. What colour were his shoes?

....

SERIES 1 – PART 2

285 In 'The Second Time Around', in what trader's magazine did Rodney say he would place an announcement concerning Del Boy's recent engagement to Pauline?

....

286 In 'The Russians are Coming', what country in Scandinavia did Rodney say the rockets were passing over during their four-minute warning test run?

....

287 In 'The Second Time Around', what did Grandad and Rodney claim Pauline was putting in Del Boy's meals to poison him?

....

288 In 'A Slow Bus to Chingford', which famous Italian artist and sculptor did Del Boy describe as a '*wally brain*'?

....

289 True or False, in 'Go West Young Man', Boycie's girlfriend crashed into the back of the Jaguar that Del Boy was driving?

....

290 In 'Christmas Crackers', Del Boy described most of Rodney's girlfriends as '*dogs*'. What type of restraint did he say Grandad found in Rodney's trousers when he took them to the cleaners?

....

291 In 'The Second Time Around', what was the nationality of the man that the old lady said Joanie Hollins married?

....

292 In 'A Slow Bus to Chingford', what type of meal did Del Boy tell Rodney was all that was required to make a big impression on his girlfriend?

....

293 In 'Christmas Crackers', Del Boy referred to the staff at the local hospital as 'A Bunch of ......'. Complete Del Boy's description.

....

294 In 'The Second Time Around', did Del Boy describe Rodney to Pauline as a 'wally', a 'divvy' or a 'big scruff'?

....

'THE LONG LEGS OF THE LAW'

295 When Grandad could not find his teeth, where did Rodney suggest he look for them?

....

296 Trigger left some items at the flat that he thought Del Boy would be interested in selling. Did he leave: paint, watches or ladies' tights?

....

297 What type of sandwich did Grandad make Del Boy?

....

298 Rodney had an upset stomach and drank, what he believed to be, a glass of ordinary water to help him. What had Grandad put in the water?

....

299 When Del Boy told Rodney that ICI had dropped a point, what was Rodney's response?

....

300 Which player did Del Boy say the team in No. 299 should never have sold?

....

301 What was the name of the policewoman that Rodney took to the pictures?

....

302 Can you recall the name of the Arnold Schwarzenegger movie Rodney took her to see?

....

303 During the scene in the café, what did Del Boy tell Sid he had had for breakfast?

....

304 Rodney said he had '...*on toast*'. Can you recall what Rodney described his scrambled eggs as?

....

NO. 1 HITS – 2

**MATCH THE SONG THAT WAS NO. I IN
THE BRITISH RECORD CHARTS WITH THE
EPISODE THAT WAS FIRST TELEVISED AT
THE SAME TIME**

	SONG	EPISODE
305	'Don't You Want Me' (1981) by The Human League	'Heroes and Villains'
306	'Mr Blobby' (1993) by Mr Blobby	'Sleeping Dogs Lie'
307	'You Spin Me Round' (1985) by Dead Or Alive	'The Jolly Boys' Outing'

308 'Knockin' On Heaven's Door'   'The Yellow Peril'
    (1996) by Dunblane

....

309 'I Know Him So Well'   'He Ain't Heavy,
    (1985) by Elaine Paige & Barbara Dickson He's My Uncle'

....

310 'Innuendo'   'Three Men, A Woman
    (1991) by Queen   And A Baby'

....

311 'I Don't Wanna Dance'   'The Long Legs
    (1982) by Eddy Grant   Of The Law'

....

312 'Pass The Dutchie'   'Christmas Crackers'
    (1982) by Musical Youth

....

313 '3am Eternal'   'Strained Relations'
    (1991) by KLF

....

314 'Do They Know It's Christmas?'   'Fatal Extraction'
    (1989) by Band Aid

....

DEL BOY – 2

315 In 'The Second Time Around', when Del Boy took a telephone call from Trigger at the flat, he could be seen wearing a Chinese dressing gown and a pair of slippers. Describe the colour and style of the slippers?

....

316 In 'Christmas Crackers', Del Boy called Rodney '*A dozy little ... ...*' Complete the description.

....

317 In 'The Long Legs of the Law', what French singer's wife did Del Boy claim wore the nylon tights he was attempting to sell in the market?

....

318 Was Del Boy a Mod or a Rocker when he was younger?

....

319　In 'A Slow Bus to Chingford', Del Boy got Rodney a job as a 'Trainee NSO'. What did Del Boy say the letters NSO stood for?

....

320　What was the first name of Del Boy and Rodney's mum?

....

321　In 'The Second Time Around', Del Boy asked Grandad to turn the TV over so he could see something on Channel 4. What did Del Boy want to watch?

....

322　In 'The Russians are Coming', Grandad claimed that the only war Del Boy ever fought was 'The ... War'. What is the missing word?

....

323　Del Boy always said that when he went out with a woman she was guaranteed three things. Name any two of them.

....

324　In 'The Long Legs of the Law', Del Boy mentioned a friend of his named Monkey. What was Monkey's surname?

....

'ASHES TO ASHES'

325 At the beginning of the episode Del Boy was attempting to sell '*Authentic French Nylon ......*'. What was he selling?

....

326 How much was he looking for per pair of the item in No. 325?

....

327 How did Del Boy describe the Mona Lisa that was hanging above the fireplace in Trigger's Gran's house?

....

328 Trigger told Del Boy he was going on holiday and claimed that he was going somewhere sunny and with lots of beaches. What country was he visiting?

....

329 What was Del Boy's response when Rodney told him that the ashes in the urn were '*Arthur's ashes*'?

....

330 Who was Arthur?

....

331 True or False, Grandad had an affair with Trigger's Granny?

....

332 Del Boy attempted to dispose of Arthur's ashes at St Katharine's Dock. Who prevented Del Boy from pouring the ashes into the River Thames?

....

333 What religion did Del Boy claim that he and Rodney were when they were confronted in No. 332?

....

334 How were Arthur's ashes eventually disposed of?

....

MIXED BAG – 5

335 In 'A Slow Bus to Chingford', Del Boy claimed that Rodney's last job had been a '*Milk ....*'. Complete the job description.

....

336 Name either of the above two cities/towns in England that Rodney said the Russian missiles were passing over in 'The Russians are Coming'.

....

337 In 'The Long Legs of the Law', Rodney mentioned that Sandra's 24-hour warning reminded him of a Gene Pitney song. However, Rodney changed the last word of the song's title. Can you recall the song and what Rodney changed the song title to?

....

338 In 'It Never Rains...', Del Boy and Rodney both called the prison guard by a different Spanish boy's name. Name any one of them.

....

339 In 'Diamonds are for Heather', what reason did Heather offer for not accepting the engagement ring that Del Boy wanted to give her?

....

340 In 'The Second Time Around', Del Boy claimed that when he was young, girls would leave their boyfriends for a bloke who had a faster what?

....

341 Was Grandad the father of Del Boy and Rodney's mum or dad?

....

342 What type of car did Rodney buy Del Boy in 'Time on Our Hands'?

....

343 In 'The Jolly Boys' Outing', name any one of the three characters that went on the Pirate Ship ride that turned them upside down.

....

344 In 'It Never Rains....', how many days did it rain non-stop?

....

'IT NEVER RAINS...'

345 It never stopped raining in Peckham, and it rained so much that Del Boy wished he had been the Chairman of a well-known raincoat manufacturer. Can you recall the company he referred to?

....

346 What type of card did Rodney purchase for Del Boy as a joke?

....

347 Del Boy persuaded the owner of the local travel agency to offer a discounted holiday to any destination in the world, but only to the next customer who walked into his shop. What percentage of the price did Del Boy persuade him to knock off?

....

348 What was the name of the owner of the travel agency: Alex, Barney or Mickey?

....

349 To what part of Spain did Del Boy book the holiday?

....

350 Why was Grandad arrested on his way back from the beach to the hotel?

....

351 Why did Grandad think he had been arrested?

....

352 What war was being fought the last time Grandad visited Spain?

....

353 When Rodney tried to explain to Grandad that he was looking for a consul what did Grandad think he was doing?

....

354 What major sporting event had just taken place in Spain prior to the Trotters' arrival?

....

CASSANDRA

355 What is Cassandra's real name?

....

356 True or False, 'Cassandra' was actually born in Peckham, London?

....

357 What other TV show did she star in with David Jason?

....

358 In what episode did we see Cassandra for the first time?

....

359 Which episode does the actress in No. 355 claim to be
    her favourite: 'Danger UXD', 'Yuppy Love' or 'The Unlucky
    Winner Is…'?

....

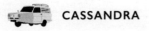

360 In 'The Unlucky Winner Is…', what did Del tell Cassandra to get waxed?

....

361 In what episode did Cassandra have a miscarriage?

....

362 What occupation did Cassandra have when she first met Rodney?

....

363 True or False, Cassandra went on a date with Mickey Pearce before she dated Rodney?

....

364 What was Cassandra's maiden name?

....

'A TOUCH OF GLASS'

365 How many of the Trotter family visited the Auction Rooms in the country?

....

366 What did Del Boy purchase a consignment of at the auction?

....

367 What song/tune did the items in No. 366 play?

....

368 Del Boy claimed that North Koreans ate dogs. He then went on to mention four meals that all had the name of a dog in them. Name any one of the breeds of dogs referred to.

....

369 Can you recall the name of the dogs home that Del Boy
claimed would be mistaken by North Korean people as a
take-away restaurant?

....

369 Can you recall the surname of the '*lady*' whose car had broken
down on a country road?

....

370 Del Boy agreed to tow the lady's car in No. 369 to her home.
When they arrived there, the butler greeted them. What was
his name?

....

371 What type of sandwich, and make of tea, did Del Boy tell Rodney
he wasn't going home without?

....

372 Rodney was warned by Del Boy not to tell his joke about the
'......... *Magician*'. By what term did Del Boy call the magician?

....

373 Did the Lord of the large country house the Trotters visited say
he had been to Oxford or Cambridge?

....

374 When the butler brought Del Boy a brandy, what type of soda
did he say they had run out of?

....

375 In 'A Touch of Glass', how much did Del Boy pay for each musical cat at the auction rooms: 75p, £1.25 or £1.75?

....

376 In 'Ashes to Ashes', what was Del Boy referring to when he pretended to be Trigger's grandfather and asked Grandad to tell him where he had hidden something?

....

377 In 'The Yellow Peril', why did Del Boy say Rodney was the best qualified of the two of them to paint the Chinese takeaway?

....

378 In 'The Long Legs of the Law', what fell out of Del Boy 's coat in the café when he learnt that Rodney was going to go on a date with a policewoman named Sandra?

....

379 In 'It Never Rains…', how did Del Boy refer to the terrorist organisation, Black September?

....

380 In 'A Touch of Glass', who did Del Boy claim to be his favourite artist when he was chatting to Lord Ridgemere in the sitting room?

....

381 In 'Ashes to Ashes', where did Grandad say the item in No. 376 was hidden?

....

382 In 'The Long Legs of the Law', Sandra claimed that she was not interested in those items that fell off the backs of lorries but that she was interested in '*Who …… them and who …….. them up*'. Can you complete the sentence with the two words that both begin with the letter 'P'.

....

383 In 'It Never Rains…', complete the following remark Del Boy made to the guard in the Spanish prison, '*Quo… *'.

....

384 In 'No Greater Love', at what disco did Del Boy tell Rodney he would probably meet a really nice girl?

....

'DIAMONDS ARE FOR HEATHER'

385 How much did Rodney pay per ticket to attend the Spanish Night that was held in The Nag's Head?

....

386 What type of business chain did Del Boy's girlfriend's father leave her when he died?

....

387 Can you recall the brand of washing powder that Del Boy purchased two tonnes of?

....

388 What area of London did Heather live in?

....

389 Del Boy described the area Heather lived in as '*Rourke's.....*' Can you complete the description?

....

390 What was the name of Heather's son: Daniel, Darren or David?

....

391 Del Boy mentioned that he had to pick up a consignment of cooking items that were fire damaged. What were they?

....

392 What rhyming-slang term did Del Boy use for his overcoat?

....

393 In this episode, Del Boy and Heather's son could be seen sporting the same baseball cap. What was written on the cap?

....

394 What type of ship did Del Boy take Heather and her little boy aboard in this episode?

....

MIKE

395 Can you name the actor who played Mike?

....

396 True or False, the actor in No. 395's father was a Scottish
heavyweight wrestling champion?

....

397 What was Mike's surname in the show: Carter, Fisher or Stevens?

....

398 Can you name the classic BBC comedy series, set in India, that
Mike starred in before securing a part in *Only Fools and Horses*?

....

MIKE

399 In what city in the northwest of England was the actor who played Mike born?

....

400 In what episode did Mike first appear?

....

401 What did Del Boy and Mike get an Irishman to do in the episode in No. 400, from which they both profited?

....

402 In what year was the episode in No. 400 first televised?

....

403 What type of car did Mike drive in 'Chain Gang'?

....

404 Mike always claimed that he had certain documents indicating the quality of his beer. What did he always maintain he had?

....

'HOMESICK'

405 When Rodney told Del Boy that Grandad was complaining about his sore legs, Del Boy said that he told Grandad not to run in '*The London* ......' What race was Del Boy speaking about?

....

406 At the beginning of the episode, Del Boy mentioned that he was going out on a date. Was he taking out: a croupier from the Casino, a hairdresser or a waitress from the Pizza Palace?

....

407 When Rodney went to the Tenants Association meeting we could only see the Chairman and Rodney in the room until one of Del Boy's mates arrived. Who sat down beside Rodney?

....

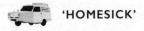

408 On the table in front of the Chairman of the Tenants Association, there were three signs. Two of the signs read, *Chairman* and *Vice-Chairman*. What was written on the third sign?

....

409 Which two positions on the committee of the Tenants Association was Rodney elected to at the meeting?

....

410 What two words did Rodney say to effectively close the meeting?

....

411 What did Del Boy tell the girl in No. 406 he did for a living: Concorde Pilot, Euro Minister or Stockbroker?

....

412 When the doctor visited Grandad at the flat, which racing horse, also the name of a Russian ballet dancer, did the doctor say Grandad had legs like?

....

413 What item of fruit was Del Boy selling at the market and could be seen all over the flat throughout the episode?

....

414 How many of the items in No. 413 was Del Boy offering to his customers in the market for 25 pence?

....

'HEALTH COMPETITION'

415 What was Del Boy attempting to sell to passers-by at the beginning of the episode: Canteens of Cutlery, Toy Puppy Dogs or Watches?

....

416 How much was Del Boy looking to get for each of the items in No. 415: £6, £7 or £8?

....

417 Why did Del Boy say he needed to sell the items in No. 415 quickly in order that he would have room in his suitcase?

....

418 In this episode Del Boy was chased by a policeman. When he got back to the flat what French word did he use to describe the policeman to Grandad?

....

419 Apart from a policeman, who else chased Del Boy through the back streets and alleys?

....

420 In this episode, how old did Rodney say he was?

....

421 Rodney decided it was time to break up his partnership with Del Boy. Who did he say he was going into business with?

....

422 What did Rodney and his new business partner in No. 421, purchase at the auction rooms?

....

423 What did Del Boy purchase at the auction rooms: cut glass goblets, fire-damaged smoke alarms or ladies' tights?

....

424 What did Rodney ask Grandad to make him to eat at the flat?

....

NO.1 HITS – 3

MATCH THE SONG THAT WAS NO. I IN THE BRITISH RECORD CHARTS AT THE SAME TIME THE EPISODE WAS FIRST TELEVISED

SONG	EPISODE
425 'Save Your Love' (1982) by Renee and Renato	'Rodney Come Home'

....

| 426 'Sadness Part 1' (1991) by Enigma | 'The Sky's The Limit' |

....

| 427 'Don't Leave Me This Way' (1986) by The Communards | 'The Frog's Legacy' |

....

428 'Saviour's Day'   'Diamonds Are For Heather'
     (1990) by Cliff Richard

....

429 'Easy Lover'   'Mother Nature's Son'
     (1985) by Philip Bailey & Phil Collins

....

430 'Always On My Mind'   'Miami Twice'
     (1987) by The Pet Shop Boys

....

431 'I Will Always Love You'   'The Miracle of Peckham'
     (1992) by Whitney Houston

....

432 'Ice Ice Baby'   'Watching the Girls Go By'
     (1990) by Vanilla Ice

....

433 'I Want To Wake Up With You'   'The Longest Night'
     (1986) by Boris Gardner

....

434 'Bohemian Rhapsody'   'The Class of '62'
     (1991) by Queen

....

MIXED BAG – 6

435 What was the first episode of Series 4: 'Chain Gang', 'Happy Returns' or 'May the Force Be with You'?

....

436 If Del Boy sold something for a 'pony' how much would he receive?

....

437 True or False, Tessa Peake-Jones (*Racquel*) also starred in *Midsomer Murders*?

....

438 In 'Big Brother', how did Rodney think Trigger got his name?

....

439 Following on from No. 438, how did Del Boy say Trigger got his name?

....

440 Buster Merryfield (*Uncle Albert*) also starred in *A Tale Of Four* ....
Can you complete this naval sounding title?

....

441 What was the name of the Tower Block where the Trotters lived?

....

442 What is the real name of the Tower Block in No. 441: Acton Tower,
Bridgewater Tower or Harlech Tower?

....

443 What is the name of the episode in which the Trotters spend
the night inside a supermarket?

....

444 True or False, we first see Del Boy and Rodney's father in
'Strained Relations'?

....

RODNEY – 2

445 What did Rodney tell Del Boy the green keeper at Peckham Bowling Club would think the club had if Del Boy left Arthur's ashes in a mound, in the episode 'Ashes to Ashes'?

....

446 How many years did Rodney spend at school?

....

447 In 'Homesick', Grandad visited Del Boy and Rodney in the market. What type of fish pie was Rodney going to be given for his tea because Del Boy said he didn't like it?

....

448 In 'A Slow Bus to Chingford', what was Rodney wearing on his feet when he was working as a night watchman?

....

449 In 'A Touch of Glass', Del Boy persuaded Rodney to help him clean the chandeliers by informing Rodney that this job and future jobs would bring them riches. Del Boy told Rodney that his shoes would be made by Gucci. Where did he say Rodney would get his clothes?

....

450 In 'Christmas Crackers', Del Boy claimed that Rodney '*had gone out with more dogs than ......*'. Can you complete the line?

....

451 In 'Diamonds are for Heather', Del Boy had a '*Del and Heather*' sun visor in the van. What did Grandad say people would think Rodney was when he was in the van with Del Boy?

....

452 In 'The Second Time Around', what type of *scratchings* did Rodney ask Del Boy to get for him at the pub?

....

453 Can you recall the name of the series that Nicholas Lyndhurst starred in after *Goodnight Sweetheart*?

....

454 Up to Series 4, how many terms had Rodney spent at the Adult Education Centre?

....

'FRIDAY THE 14TH'

455 What type of equipment was Del Boy carrying and wearing when he burst into the flat?

....

456 When Grandad saw Del Boy with the items in No. 455 he asked Del Boy where they were going. What did Del Boy say they were going to do with the equipment at first?

....

457 Whose weekend cottage were the Trotters going to stay at?

....

458 Where in the south of England was the cottage situated?

....

459 Who were the boys stopped by on their way to the cottage?

....

460 When they arrived at the cottage there was a storm blowing.
     How did Del Boy describe the weather, leading him to ask
     Rodney to put the kettle on and make a cup of tea after Rodney
     corrected his pronunciation of the word?

....

461 What type of alcohol did Del Boy ask Rodney to search for in
     the sideboard?

....

462 Rodney discovered an axe and a board game in the sideboard?
     What board game did he find?

....

463 Who paid the boys a visit at the cottage?

....

464 Who did the person in No. 463 say he really was?

....

'YESTERDAY NEVER COMES'

465   Can you recall the name of the '*Queen*' that Del Boy said the cabinet he purchased was named after: Queen Anne, Queen Elizabeth or Queen Victoria?

....

466   What did Rodney say the cabinet had?

....

467   When Del Boy said he was thinking of getting the British Museum to look at the cabinet, who did Rodney suggest should take a look?

....

468   What was the Christian name of the antique dealer who examined the cabinet in the flat: Mandy, Melissa or Miranda?

....

469 How did Grandad refer to the person in No. 468?

....

470 In what area of London was the antique dealer's shop located?

....

471 When Del Boy and Rodney examined the cabinet, they noticed writing on the inside of it. What type of box did the antique dealer say part of the cabinet had been made from?

....

472 Where did Del Boy slap the antique dealer before asking her out for a curry?

....

473 What happened to Rodney the following day when he attempted a similar action as Del Boy had done in No. 472?

....

474 Who owned the painting that caught the attention of the antique dealer in the flat?

....

475 In 'No Greater Love', what did Rodney see on the mantelpiece of the lady's house he visited that distracted him from the confident mood he was in?

....

476 In 'A Losing Streak', Del Boy described the colour of the mink coat as 'mottle grey with highlights'. What two colours made up the highlights?

....

477 In 'Ashes to Ashes', Rodney got into a bit of trouble with his girlfriend's father because there was something wrong with the way he was wearing his jeans. Can you recall what the problem was?

....

478 In 'It Never Rains…', what did Del Boy think a *Spanish Pension* was?

....

479 In 'The Long Legs of the Law', who did the policewoman that Rodney was dating say she was bringing around to the flat the next day: CID, The Fraud Squad or MI5?

....

480 In 'A Touch of Glass', what make did Lady Ridgemere say most of her fine porcelain china was?

....

481 In 'The Yellow Peril', what did Del Boy suggest Rodney should do with his paintbrush so that it would fit into the small tins of paint?

....

482 In 'Ashes to Ashes', when Grandad asked Rodney to examine the urn, why was Rodney reluctant to do so at first?

....

483 In 'A Touch of Glass', what word beginning with the letter 'P', did Rodney call Wallace, the butler?

....

484 In 'It Never Rains…', what type of *bomb* did Del Boy tell Rodney he would like to send their dad for Father's Day?

....

'MAY THE FORCE BE WITH YOU'

485 Who did we see Rodney speaking to in The Nag's Head at the start of the episode?

....

486 What colour did Trigger say the hat he told Rodney he had lost was:

    green, pink or purple?

....

487 Trigger met an old school mate named Roy Slater in the pub. What rank was Slater in the police?

....

488 What stolen item did Slater ask Trigger about?

....

106

489 When Boycie joined Trigger and Slater in the pub, Slater mentioned to Boycie that he had heard he was involved in pirate tapes. Boycie tried to play it down by mentioning two pirate movies. Name either of them.

....

490 What did Grandad think the item in No. 488 was?

....

491 When Slater visited Del Boy at the flat, who did Del Boy say Grandad was?

....

492 True or False, Slater arrested his own father for having a defective light on his bike?

....

493 Following the theme in No. 489, when Slater asked Del Boy about Boycie, what did Del Boy say Boycie had at his house, and therefore Slater could not miss it?

....

494 How did Slater describe the illegal substance Rodney had been caught and charged with possession of when he was at art college?

....

MIXED BAG – 7

495 In 'Cash and Curry', what type of Ford did the two Indian gentlemen drive away in at the end of the episode?

....

496 In 'Diamonds are for Heather', where did Del Boy give Heather an engagement ring?

....

497 What type of pie did Auntie make for Del Boy, Grandad and Rodney in 'The Second Time Around'?

....

498 In 'A Touch of Glass', where did Del Boy, Grandad and Rodney first meet Lady Ridgemere?

....

499 Complete Del Boy's quip from the episode 'A Slow Bus to
Chingford': '*Allemagne ...... points*'.

....

500 After setting up '*Trotters Ethnic Tours*' in 'A Slow Bus to Chingford',
Del Boy gave everyone a role in the new company: Rodney would
drive the bus while Grandad would sell programmes. What role did
Del Boy give himself?

....

501 In a famous line from 'Go West Young Man' a girl asked Rodney
if he preferred Grass or Astro Turf. What was Rodney's response?

....

502 In 'A Touch of Glass', when the Trotters stopped to assist Lady
Ridgemere, which Formula 1 racing team did Del Boy claim he
used to drive for?

....

503 In 'The Second Time Around', did Del Boy claim that most of
Rodney's dates arrived at the flat by school bus, skateboard
or taxi?

....

504 In 'Cash and Curry', complete Del Boy's line: '*As Macbeth said
to .... in* A Midsummer Night's Dream'.

....

505 How did Del Boy refer to the twin sisters that Mickey and Rodney were contemplating chatting up in The Nag's Head?

....

506 On his way home from The Nag's Head, Rodney met a woman sitting on a wall. Who or what was she waiting for?

....

507 What did the woman in No. 506 call Rodney when he first spoke to her?

....

508 Do you recall what the woman screamed at Rodney that resulted in him running away?

....

509 What did Rodney claim to be when the woman accused him of touching her?

....

510 Who told Del Boy that Rodney had '*gone on the run*'?

....

511 Where did Boycie suggest Del Boy looked for Rodney in case he was hiding there?

....

512 Can you recall the location of Rodney's hiding place?

....

513 What did Rodney bring with him to eat at his hideout?

....

514 What '*House*' did Del Boy tell Rodney had been burnt to the ground?

....

'WHO'S A PRETTY BOY?'

515 Del Boy gave Rodney a sign to place over the parking meter outside The Nag's Head. What was written on it?

....

516 Can you remember the Christian name of the Irishman who sold Del Boy some paint?

....

517 What colour of paint did the man in No. 516 sell to Del Boy, pretending that it was white?

....

518 Who did the Irishman say he was looking for when he was chatting to Del Boy in the pub?

....

519 What type of bird did Denzil and his wife keep at his flat?

....

520 What colour was the bird in No. 519?

....

521 What type of fruit did Del Boy lift from the fruit bowl and proceed
to eat in Denzil's flat?

....

522 Denzil asked Del Boy to do some work for him? What did Denzil
pay Del Boy to do?

....

523 Del Boy claimed that Rodney was so white in colour that
'*what looked bronzer than him*'?

....

524 What happened to the bird in No. 519?

....

'THICKER THAN WATER'

525 Which member of the Trotter Family opened the door of the flat when Del Boy's and Rodney's father, Reggie, turned up at Christmas in this episode?

....

526 Who was Rodney speaking about when he told Grandad that 'it took Del two weeks to get her out of quarantine'?

....

527 How many years had it been since Del Boy, Grandad and Rodney had seen their father?

....

528 In what part of northeast England had Reggie been living prior to visiting the boys?

....

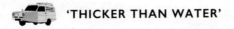

529 Reggie claimed to be ill. What did he say the nature of his illness was?

....

530 What fruit drink did Del Boy order as a mixer with his Grand Marnier in The Nag's Head?

....

531 What drink did Del Boy purchase his father, Grandad and Rodney in the pub?

....

532 Whose bed did Reggie sleep in when he stayed at the flat?

....

533 Where did Reggie take Rodney to make up for the time he missed spending with Rodney when he was growing up?

....

534 When Del Boy returned to the flat, what did he ask Grandad to put under the grill for him to eat?

....

MIXED BAG - 8

535 In 'A Slow Bus to Chingford', did Del Boy claim to be a Byzantine Man, a Contemporary Man or a Renaissance Man?

....

536 In 'A Touch of Glass', how did Lady Ridgemere's butler get her car around to the back of the house?

....

537 In 'Friday The 14th', the mad axe killer asked Del Boy if he liked fish. Del Boy told him that he did but mentioned that he liked fish with two other things. Name the two things.

....

538 In 'Yesterday Never Comes', with who did Del Boy think Rodney had been playing marbles?

....

539 In 'Cash and Curry', the Indian gentlemen claimed to be descended from two different types of 'caste'. Can you recall the castes concerned?

....

540 In 'The Second Time Around', what did Trigger tell Del Boy that Pauline's ex-husband had died of?

....

541 In 'The Russians are Coming', what did Del Boy borrow from the nearby building site for the shelter when they were having a trial '*Nuclear Alert*' run?

....

542 In 'Diamonds are for Heather', on how many weeks approval did Del Boy take out the engagement ring?

....

543 In 'Homesick', what show did Grandad want to see only for him to collapse on the floor before he could switch channels?

....

544 In 'Healthy Competition', where did Del Boy say the girl that Mickey Pearce had met on holiday came from?

....

545 Can you recall the African country that Del Boy claimed the mink coat he was selling came from?

....

546 What *colour* (clue: *cat*) did Rodney describe the mink coat as?

....

547 Who did Trigger tell Rodney that Del Boy had lost money playing cards with the previous evening?

....

548 How much did Trigger say Del Boy had lost: £100, £150 or £200?

....

549 What '*lucky charm*' did Del Boy say he had with him when he lost the money in No. 548?

....

550 What did Grandad give Del Boy for good luck?

....

551 Del Boy organised a poker night at his flat. Name the two people he played cards with in the flat?

....

552 When Del Boy told Rodney about the time their dad walked out and left them, he said he remembered it clearly because it was his birthday. What birthday did he say it was?

....

553 Grandad claimed that Boycie knew more card tricks than a British magician who had recently appeared in a beer advertisement. Name the magician.

....

554 When Del Boy was struggling to match Boycie's bet in the final card game, what did Trigger give him as capital?

....

'NO GREATER LOVE'

555   Name any one of the main two items that Del Boy and Rodney
were selling in this episode?

....

556   Can you remember the surname of the Asian lady's house that
Del Boy sent Rodney to, for the purposes of collecting some
money she owed Del Boy?

....

557   To where in Asia did the new occupier of the house in No. 556
tell Rodney the lady had moved?

....

558   Rodney fell in love with an older woman. What was her Christian
name: Carmel, Denise or Irene?

....

559 Where was the husband of Rodney's new love?

....

560 How old did Rodney tell Del Boy his new love was?

....

561 When Rodney asked Del Boy if he should confront his new love's
husband, what part of his body did Del Boy tell Rodney he might
end up getting re-arranged?

....

562 Del Boy told Grandad that Rodney had fallen in and out of love
more times than a very famous American detective duo. Name the
TV cops.

....

563 When Rodney's new love's son spoke to Del Boy in The Nag's
Head, Rodney was curious as to how he knew Del Boy's name.
Del Boy tried to say that it was because he had a gold 'D' hanging
around his neck. Name any two of the three Christian names
Rodney said the 'D' could have stood for.

....

564 What did Del Boy call the punk rockers that were at the bar in
The Nag's Head?

....

'THE YELLOW PERIL'

565 'The Golden…'. Complete the car-sounding name of the Chinese takeaway in this episode.

....

566 Can you recall the name of the owner of the Chinese takeaway? (Clue: *His surname can be found on the body.*)

....

567 What job did Del Boy agree to do at the Chinese takeaway?

....

568 When the owner of the Chinese takeaway discussed payment for the job in No. 567, what credit card did he ask Del Boy whether he took?

....

569 Del Boy and Rodney visited the cemetery to sit beside their mum's grave. The monument on her grave was so big that what did Rodney say it needed when it was erected?

....

570 When Del Boy opened the door of the Chinese takeaway, what ran out?

....

571 What did Del Boy say when he was saying goodbye to the owner of the Chinese takeaway after agreeing to do a job there: *Sianora*, *Pagoda* or *Beijing*?

....

572 What type of watch did Rodney ask Del Boy for when Del Boy told him that he would share half of everything he owned with Rodney?

....

573 How much did Del Boy receive for the job in No. 567?

....

574 How was the money from No. 573 shared out between Del Boy, Rodney and Grandad?

....

'HAPPY RETURNS'

575 What name did Rodney give to the pornographic magazine that he asked Del Boy to get for him in the newsagents?

....

576 Why would Rodney not ask for the magazine himself?

....

577 When Del Boy and Rodney prevented a young boy from running out in front of an oncoming car, Del Boy asked the boy if he had ever heard of something. What was it?

....

578 How much did Del Boy give the little boy to get himself an ice cream?

....

579 Why was the little boy's mother so angry with him?

....

580 When Del Boy met the little boy later he took him home to his mum.
As it turned out, Del used to be engaged to the mother of the boy.
What was her name: Jeanie, Jenny or Junie ?

....

581 When Del Boy was at the flat of his former fiancée, Rodney walked
in the door. What was he doing there?

....

582 Rodney had a bottle of brandy and an LP with him when he arrived.
Can you recall the name of the pop group and album title of the
LP he was carrying?

....

583 Later in the episode, Del Boy learned that the girl in No. 576, was
celebrating her birthday by holding a birthday party the following
week. How old would she be?

....

584 What did Mickey Pearce tell Del Boy he was learning at evening
school that prompted Del Boy to ask Mickey to 'say something
in it'?

....

'STRAINED RELATIONS'

585 What did Del Boy give Rodney to throw into Grandad's grave?

....

586 Who owned the item in No. 585?

....

587 Who were we led to believe broke into The Nag's Head and stole the cigarette machine?

....

588 What '*hot car items*' did Del Boy ask Rodney to put in the hall until all the funeral guests had left the flat?

....

589 From what part of London did Del Boy's relatives, who turned up at the funeral, come from: North, South or West?

....

590 What member of the Trotter Family attended Grandad's funeral with Del Boy's cousin and his wife?

....

591 After the funeral Del Boy and Rodney were in the flat and Del Boy made them their tea. Del Boy made sausages and mash. Why did Rodney say he couldn't eat it?

....

592 When Rodney thought that Del Boy was not mourning Grandad's death sufficiently, Del Boy was angry with him. What children's TV character did Del Boy claim to '*have more bounce than*'?

....

593 What did Mike say he was going to do as a mark of respect for Grandad?

....

594 Del Boy told Rodney that when Grandad was younger he learned how to cook at one of London's largest establishments. What type of establishment was Del Boy referring to?

....

'HOLE IN ONE'

595 What '*hole*' did Uncle Albert fall down?

....

596 Rodney went to the auction rooms to purchase some merchandise for the business. Despite the fact that it was freezing cold at the time, what did Rodney purchase?

....

597 How much did Rodney spend on the items in No. 596?

....

598 Rodney blamed Uncle Albert for his and Del Boy's recent misfortune. What did Rodney refer to Uncle Albert as?

....

599 When Rodney, Del Boy and Uncle Albert were sitting in The Nag's Head, Rodney was attempting to work out how they could raise some money for the business. What type of equations did he say he did at school that would help them?

....

600 When Uncle Albert fell down the 'hole' in No. 595, what did Rodney say he had probably broken?

....

601 Can you recall the name of the solicitor Del Boy engaged to

represent Uncle Albert in Court?

....

602 When Del Boy was giving evidence in Court what '*Jimmy of Peckham*' did he describe Uncle Albert as prior to his accident?

....

603 What 'hole' did Del Boy claim was probably the only hole Uncle Albert had not fallen down in his life?

....

604 What explanation did Uncle Albert offer as the reason why he fell down the hole?

....

'IT'S ONLY ROCK 'N' ROLL'

605 In this episode Rodney was a member of a rock 'n' roll band. What was his role in the band?

....

606 What nickname did Del Boy give Rodney based on No. 605?

....

607 Do you remember what name Del Boy referred to the band as, a name the band later adopted as their own?

....

608 What type of damaged girl's toy was Del Boy attempting to shift?

....

609 What country were the toys in No. 608 made in: Malaysia, North Korea or Taiwan?

....

610 Del Boy got Rodney's band a booking to play at a local club. Can you name the Irish club where the band had been booked to play on St Patrick's Night?

....

611 What famous pop group at the time did Del Boy say the band had not quite reached the standard of?

....

612 After Rodney left the band they appeared on a famous TV show. Name the show.

....

613 What was the name of the song that the band sang on the TV show mentioned in No. 612: 'Boys, Boys, Yeah, Yeah'; 'Boys Will Be Boys' or 'Boys Just Want To Have Fun'?

....

614 Can you recall the nickname given to the lead singer of the band by Del Boy?

....

MIXED BAG – 9

615 In 'Hole in One', what did Del Boy say Uncle Albert probably had as result of flying through the air after he fell into the cellar at The Nag's Head?

....

616 In 'Strained Relations', Uncle Albert went into The Nag's Head for lunch. What was on the menu that he claimed had put him off eating?

....

617 In 'Happy Returns', who brought Debbie home when Del Boy went to see Junie for the second time?

....

618 In 'Wanted', what did Del Boy say Grandad was calling everyone after inhaling some of the smoke from Rodney's tobacco mix via the air ducts in the flat?

....

619 In 'May the Force Be with You', Del Boy asked Slater what charge he was going to fit up Grandad with. What forged item did Del Boy mention?

....

620 In 'Yesterday Never Comes', Del Boy claimed that Rodney had more nose than a certain Walt Disney character. Name the character.

....

621 In 'Friday The 14th', what was the make of glue that Del Boy asked Grandad and Rodney whether they had been sniffing?

....

622 In 'Healthy Competition', Del Boy couldn't believe that Rodney failed to recognise a police car. Name either of the two descriptions that Del Boy gave the police car.

....

623 In 'Homesick', Del Boy told the lady in charge of Housing and Welfare that he was considering purchasing some tickets to see a Russian ballet dancer, only to be told that the ballet dancer had died in 1950. Name the ballet dancer.

....

624 In a famous quip from 'A Touch of Glass', Del Boy claimed that asking a Trotter what they knew about chandeliers was like asking a certain person what they knew about cakes. What '*famous baker*' did Del Boy mention by name?

....

'SLEEPING DOGS LIE'

625 When Rodney told Uncle Albert that he moved the television aerial because he noticed a ghost on the TV screen, what type of film did Uncle Albert say he was watching?

....

626 Boycie and Marlene were going on holiday and Del Boy agreed to look after their dog for them whilst they were away? Where did Boycie say they were going on holiday?

....

627 How much did Del Boy charge Boycie per week for looking after the dog?

....

628 What was the dog's name: Charlie, Dukie or Lucky?

....

629 What breed was the dog?

....

630 What did Marlene tell Del Boy not to forget to give to the dog every morning before his breakfast?

....

631 When Del Boy and Rodney took the dog to the park for some exercise, what did Del Boy try to sell to the lady he met out walking her dog, after she complained to Del Boy about what her dog kept doing at home?

....

632 What meat did Del Boy and Rodney feed the dog for breakfast the day they had to take him to the vet for a check-up?

....

633 Why did Uncle Albert have to go to hospital for tests?

....

634 When Marlene asked to speak to the dog over the telephone, what did Del Boy call her: *Dozy Mare, Scatty Mare or Silly Mare*?

....

'WATCHING THE GIRLS GO BY'

635 The opening scene takes us to The Nag's Head. Who was Del Boy
playing cards with?

....

636 When Rodney entered the pub what eating-place did he ask
Mickey Pearce if he was going to later on that evening?

....

637 The Nag's Head were organising a Party Evening. How much
were the tickets?

....

638 How much did Rodney bet Mickey Pearce that he was bringing
a girl to the party at The Nag's Head?

....

639 What animal did Del Boy mention when he told Rodney that
      Mickey Pearce was doing too much bragging and never shut up?

....

640 When Rodney got dressed for the party, what colour was his
      jacket and the shirt and tie that he was wearing?

....

641 Can you recall the name of the sweet that Del Boy said Rodney
      looked like?

....

642 During a discussion in the flat about 'love', Uncle Albert said that
      the Trotters wore their hearts on their sleeves. Where did Del Boy
      claim Rodney wore his heart?

....

643 What was the Christian name of the German girl Uncle Albert told
      Del Boy and Rodney he once fell in love with?

....

644 How did Rodney end up getting a date to take to the party at
      The Nag's Head?

....

'AS ONE DOOR CLOSES'

645   What item was at the centre of Del Boy's big money-making scheme in this episode?

....

646   How much, to the nearest £1,000, did Del Boy require to clinch the deal in No. 645?

....

647   When Del Boy was struggling to get the money for his latest get-rich quick venture, Rodney came up with an idea after reading an article in a newspaper supplement. What creature did Rodney say he had been reading about?

....

648   What types of combs was Del Boy selling in the market, advising his customers that they were the latest 'thing' in hairdressing?

....

649 How much, per item, was Del Boy charging for the items in
No. 648: £1.50, £2.00 or £2.50?

....

650 Which one of Del Boy's mates lent him £2,000?

....

651 From where did the person in No. 650 get the money?

....

652 Del Boy claimed that the item he was selling in the market was
a safer bet than putting your money on the favourite in a horse
race with a very famous jockey riding it. Which jockey was he
speaking about?

....

653 When Del Boy, Rodney and Uncle Albert were sitting in the
graveyard, Del Boy was pointing out where the members of the
Trotter family were buried. Who did Uncle Albert say he was with,
and who would look after his funeral, when he died?

....

654 When Del Boy was talking about his luck he claimed that if
someone made a film about it, that it would be more of a
tear-jerker than which 1970s' film?

....

'TO HULL AND BACK'

655 In the opening scene we see a plane landing on the runway. What European city had the plane just arrived from?

....

656 What energy drink did Rodney order with Del Boy's Tia Maria in The Nag's Head?

....

657 What items was Del Boy trying to sell in The Nag's Head and later in the Episode in the market?

....

658 In what Asian country did Del Boy claim the items in No. 657 were manufactured?

....

659 How much was Del Boy charging for the items in No. 657: £15, £20 or £25?

....

660 Del Boy had a meeting with two people in a back room at The Nag's Head? One was Boycie, who was the other person?

....

661 What did the two people in No. 660 want Del Boy to do for them?

....

662 Who joined Rodney at the bar claiming he was '*on the pull*' that evening?

....

663 How much was initially offered to Del Boy to undertake the work outlined in No. 661?

....

664 What rank did Roy Slater say he was when he ran into Del Boy and Rodney in the market?

....

'FROM PRUSSIA WITH LOVE'

665 What nationality did Rodney think the girl in The Nag's Head was when Mike told Del Boy she was foreign?

....

666 What language did Mike ask Del Boy to speak to the girl in?

....

667 What nationality was the girl?

....

668 What was her Christian name: Anna, Helga or Steffi?

....

669 Who brought her back to the flat to stay the night?

....

670 What type of student was the girl: art, drama or language?

....

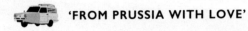
671 When Del Boy first spoke to the girl, which one of his foreign phrases did he use?

....

672 When the boys eventually discovered the girl's nationality, what type of vegetable did Del Boy say the girl had been lumbered with when Rodney decided to help her out?

....

673 When Del Boy noticed that the girl was pregnant, and found out that she intended to have her baby adopted when it was born, what plans did he have for the baby?

....

674 Which famous tennis player did Del Boy claim was the girl's cousin?

....

'THE MIRACLE OF PECKHAM'

675 What type of musical instrument did Rodney bring back to the flat from a night's drinking at The Nag's Head?

....

676 Rodney told Uncle Albert about how beautiful the girl was that he met at The Nag's Head and described her as looking like an actress who starred in Dynasty. Can you name the actress or the character she played?

....

677 Del Boy described the girl that Rodney had been with the night before as having a face that '*launched a 1,000*' what?

....

678 What did Uncle Albert do with the musical instrument in No. 675?

....

679 What did Rodney pour all over Uncle Albert's breakfast much to the displeasure of Del Boy?

....

680 Where was Del Boy going when he left the flat and told Rodney that he could have the morning off?

....

681 What made Del Boy decide to make a visit to the location in No. 680?

....

682 What local building did Del Boy offer to help raise funds to repair and thereby prevent it from closing?

....

683 How much was needed to prevent the closure of the building in No. 682: £250,000, £500,000 or £1,000,000?

....

684 When Rodney finally retrieved the musical instrument it was all bent. Who did Rodney say it looked as though had had a go at it?

....

'THE LONGEST NIGHT'

685 What amount of money did the poster at the supermarket say the one-millionth visitor to the store would win?

....

686 Why were Del Boy, Rodney and Uncle Albert stopped when they left the store by the supermarket's head of security?

....

687 Where were Del Boy, Rodney and Uncle Albert taken after being stopped?

....

688 What frozen food items did the shoplifter put down his T-shirt only to remove them again because they were too cold?

....

689 What nickname did the shoplifter inform Del Boy the police had given him?

....

690 At what time did the time-lock mechanism for the supermarket's safe switch on at, resulting in foiling the shoplifter's attempted robbery of the store?

....

691 Approximately how much cash was in the safe: £50,000, £60,000 or £70,000?

....

692 What did Uncle Albert pretend to be suffering from in an attempt to distract the shoplifter?

....

693 What two people helped plan the attempted robbery of the supermarket's safe along with the shoplifter?

....

694 From where did the shoplifter get the gun he was carrying?

....

'TEA FOR THREE'

695 Who described the beer in The Nag's Head as tasting like water: Boycie, Denzil or Trigger?

....

696 Who did Uncle Albert inform Del Boy and Rodney had just been rushed into hospital?

....

697 Whose niece paid him a visit at The Nag's Head, causing Del Boy and Rodney to almost fight over her?

....

698 What type of contest, much to Del Boy's annoyance, was taking place in the pub?

....

 **'TEA FOR THREE'**

699 Who won the contest in No. 698?

....

700 When Del Boy and Rodney were pushing one another to get to the person in No. 697, what did Del Boy tell Rodney was on the floor of the pub in attempt to distract him?

....

701 What type of home '*health machine*' did Del Boy have at the flat?

....

702 What did Rodney purchase for the special tea that was arranged at the flat?

....

703 What did Rodney arrange for Del Boy to do in the country by pretending to the person in No. 697 that Del Boy would really like it for a birthday present?

....

704 What army regiment did Del Boy pretend that he used to be a member of?

....

MIXED BAG – 10

705 In 'A Losing Streak', Trigger said that a losing streak was like being a member of a certain religious sect. Can you recall the sect he mentioned?

....

706 In 'No Greater Love', what did Irene ask Rodney when she saw him in his camel hair coat that was several sizes too big for him?

....

707 In 'The Yellow Peril', what did Del Boy say he would let Rodney borrow that persuaded Rodney to paint the kitchen of the Chinese takeaway?

....

708 In 'Homesick', what did Del Boy claim you were guaranteed not to catch if you sucked one of the oranges he was selling?

....

709 In 'Tea For Three', what did Trigger say was wrong with the wheelchair that his Granny used in an effort to make Del Boy feel better about being in a wheelchair?

....

710 In 'Healthy Competition', what did Del Boy do with the tea cosies he was struggling to sell?

....

711 In 'Friday The 14th', how did the Mad Axe Killer manage to escape from the institute for the criminally insane?

....

712 In 'Happy Returns', name any two of the three animals that Del Boy mentioned in conversation to Mickey Pearce when Mickey claimed he had a fight with five men?

....

713 In 'From Prussia With Love', what did Uncle Albert say to Anna when Del Boy asked him to ask her what her name was?

....

714 In 'Homesick', Del Boy claimed that you needed a large number of children and a particular accent to get a bungalow. What type of accent did he mention?

....

'VIDEO NASTY'

715 In the opening scene what two characters were playing cards in The Nag's Head?

....

716 For who was Mickey Pearce delivering and picking up video tapes?

....

717 What council gave Rodney a grant to make a local community film?

....

718 Who did Rodney appoint as his director for the making of the local community film?

....

719 What did Del Boy say the person in No. 718 wouldn't be able to direct to the coast, referring to his lack of film direction skills?

....

720 What did Del Boy obtain for Rodney to assist him with writing a story for the film?

....

721 When Rodney told Del Boy that he was struggling to come up with a script for the film, Del Boy told him about an idea that he thought would make a good film. What animal was involved in Del Boy's story?

....

722 When Del Boy discovered that Rodney had film-making equipment, he named two church ceremonies that he charged people to have filmed. What were they?

....

723 How much did Del Boy charge for the filming in No. 722: £50, £60 or £70?

....

724 What did Del Boy describe Boycie as when he discovered that the reason why Boycie and Marlene were finding it difficult to start a family was as a result of Boycie having a low sperm count?

....

DEL BOY – 3

725 In 'A Losing Streak', Del Boy said that Boycie had more *front* than an English seaside resort. Can you recall the resort he mentioned?

....

726 In 'The Yellow Peril', what did Rodney say Del Boy would pinch the hole out of from his mouth if he didn't keep his mouth closed?

....

727 In 'The Miracle of Peckham', what biblical film, starring Charlton Heston as Moses, did Del Boy claim he watched on TV when the priest was enquiring as to whether or not Del Boy was a Roman Catholic?

....

728 In 'Homesick', the lady in charge of Housing and Welfare said that when she was younger she wanted to be a choreographer. What type of profession did Del Boy think she was talking about?

....

729 In 'Yesterday Never Comes', how much did Del Boy initially say he was going to offer the cabinet in the paper for: £95, £105 or £115?

....

730 In 'May the Force Be with You', what Muppet character's name did Del Boy use as slang for the toilet?

....

731 In 'Wanted', Del Boy reckoned that the twin sisters Rodney and Mickey were about to chat up in The Nag's Head reminded him of a Walt Disney character. Name the character.

....

732 In 'Happy Returns', Junie invited Del Boy into her flat. Who did Junie say she was afraid her neighbours would think Del Boy was?

....

733 In 'Strained Relations', Del Boy and Rodney entered the pub and upon noticing them, Uncle Albert coughed. What store did Del Boy then say it was a pity wasn't open?

....

734 In 'The Yellow Peril', what Scandinavian country did Del Boy tell Mr Chin led the world in paint technology?

....

RODNEY – 3

735 In 'A Slow Bus to Chingford', did Rodney's girlfriend's brother work for the council, London Underground or a mini-cab firm?

....

736 In 'No Greater Love', when Rodney asked Irene out, he assumed she would say no and he mentioned two excuses that she might use. Can you recall either excuse that Rodney claimed Irene might be doing to prevent her from going out with him?

....

737 In 'Homesick', where in France did Rodney suggest they take Grandad to be cured of his illness?

....

738 In 'Yesterday Never Comes', did Rodney call the girl who slapped him in the restaurant a Fascist or a Nazi?

....

739 In 'Wanted', after learning that Rodney claimed to be a doctor, what did Del Boy ask Rodney whether he gave the woman?

....

740 In 'Hole in One', what had Uncle Albert been reading about to prompt Del Boy to say that Rodney couldn't give it away let alone sell it?

....

741 In 'Sleeping Dogs Lie', what did Rodney get Uncle Albert to eat when he was in hospital, only for him and Del Boy to eat them instead?

....

742 In 'Watching the Girls Go By', what breed of dog did Rodney say would look good on Uncle Albert?

....

743 In 'As One Door Closes', what did Rodney fear he was losing early in life?

....

744 In 'The Miracle of Peckham', what did Rodney describe Del Boy as after he claimed to have seen a miracle: a plonker, a prophet or a psychic?

....

UNCLE ALBERT – 2

745 In 'Strained Relations', how long had Uncle Albert been living with Del Boy's cousin and his wife: 14 months, 16 months or 18 months?

....

746 In 'Hole in One', where did Rodney suggest to Del Boy they could hide a barrel of beer after Uncle Albert asked Mike about the deep-fat fryer?

....

747 In 'Sleeping Dogs Lie', what did Uncle Albert take by mistake in place of his sleeping pills?

....

748. In 'Watching the Girls Go By', what German word did Uncle Albert say always reminded him of Helga when he heard it said in a German war film?

....

749 In 'The Miracle of Peckham', what was Uncle Albert eating for breakfast before Rodney sprinkled Del Boy's aftershave all over it?

....

750 In 'Video Nasty', Uncle Albert said that Rodney got the biro whereas Mickey Pearce got the .... What item did Uncle Albert say Mickey got?

....

751 In 'Strained Relations', what job did Del Boy tell Mike was Uncle Albert's last job on a ship?

....

752 In 'Hole in One', how much was the out-of-court settlement that the brewery offered Uncle Albert?

....

753 In 'Sleeping Dogs Lie', when Uncle Albert was being discharged from hospital, what did Del Boy tell Rodney not to throw at Uncle Albert?

....

754 In 'The Miracle of Peckham', what singer's album did Rodney tell Uncle Albert that Del Boy had taken the cassette tape of to church?

....

DEL BOY'S PALS

755 In 'A Losing Streak', what type of poker did Boycie, Del Boy and Trigger play?

....

756 In 'The Yellow Peril', from where did Trigger and his pal get the paint that he sold Del Boy?

....

757 In 'May the Force Be with You', which one of Del Boy's mates was the first person Slater mentioned when he asked Del Boy who stole the microwave oven?

....

758 In 'Happy Returns', why were Trigger and Rodney so convinced that Debbie was not Del Boy's daughter?

....

759   In 'Hole in One', what US City Council did Solly Atwell tell Del Boy had been sued for $30 million in a negligence case?

....

760   In 'As One Door Closes', what was Denzil wearing on his feet when he met Del Boy in the market?

....

761   In 'The Miracle of Peckham', when Del Boy telephoned Rodney and told him that he had seen a miracle, which one of Del Boy's mates did Rodney think had just bought a round of drinks?

....

762   In 'Tea for Three', which two of Del Boy's mates brought him back to the flat from the hospital?

....

763   In 'Video Nasty', how many years of marriage were Boycie and Marlene celebrating by throwing a party at The Nag's Head?

....

764   In 'May the Force Be with You', what type of lager did Del Boy give Slater to drink in the flat?

....

765 In 'Homesick', did the Doctor say Grandad was suffering from exhaustion, high blood pressure or arthritis?

....

766 In 'Healthy Competition', when Rodney discovered that Mickey Pearce had gone to Spain, he tried to hide his embarrassment by claiming that they were going into the self-catering trade. What type of house did Grandad ask Rodney if they owned in lieu of the fact that they only had £200?

....

767 In 'Friday The 14th', what song could we hear as the boys were driving on the motorway towards Cornwall?

....

768 In 'Yesterday Never Comes', what type of luxury car was parked outside Miranda's Antiques Shop when Del Boy pulled up in the three-wheel van?

....

769 In 'May The Force Be With You', Slater described the person who stole the microwave oven as '*The Phantom Of The* ....'. Complete the description.

....

770 In 'Wanted', what was Grandad going 'up West' to collect after Del Boy informed him that he had won the pools?

....

771 In 'Homesick', what war did Grandad say his Grandad had fought in?

....

772 In 'Healthy Competition', where at Mickey's house did they store the broken lawnmower engines?

....

773 In 'Friday The 14th', how much did Del Boy say they had to pay the gamekeeper in order to poach?

....

774 In 'Yesterday Never Comes', what did it say on the sign that was on the door of one of the lifts in the lobby of Nelson Mandela House?

....

775 In 'Happy Returns', what did Del Boy call the little boy when he was sitting at the side of the road: Champ, Mucker or Tiger?

....

776 In 'Strained Relations', how many times did we discover Uncle Albert had been aboard a ship that had been dive bombed in peacetime?

....

777 In 'Hole in One', name any one of the two things Del Boy said the other market traders would be selling to combat the cold weather while he and Rodney had to shift suntan lotion?

....

778 In 'Sleeping Dogs Lie', what type of animal did Uncle Albert say they could train to do the same things that Rodney could?

....

779 In 'Watching the Girls Go By', Del Boy told Rodney that he had no chance of pulling a girl if he went out '*dressed like Bertie ....*'. Can you recall the surname Del Boy mentioned?

....

780 In 'As One Door Closes', what type of popular chocolate-bar wrapper did Del Boy say they would end up chasing down Peckham High Street in search of a rare butterfly?

....

781 In 'Happy Returns', what did Junie first tell Del Boy her husband was working on?

....

782 In 'Strained Relations', why did Del Boy say there was no chance of getting Uncle Albert a taxi back to Del Boy's cousin's place given that it was such a late hour?

....

783 In 'Hole in One', as what court document did Del Boy say a £5 note would fall to earth if he threw one up in the air?

....

784 In 'Sleeping Dogs Lie', what leg did Rodney say he felt guilty about eating when he discovered Dukie wasn't well?

....

TRIGGER

785 What did Trigger always call Rodney?

....

786 In 'If They Could See Us now!', what reason did Trigger give
Rodney for calling at the flat?

....

787 What was Trigger's occupation?

....

788 True or False, Trigger lived in Nelson Mandela House?

....

789 In 'Tea for Three' what relationship was Trigger to the girl that
Del Boy and Rodney were arguing over in The Nag's Head?

....

790. In 'The Jolly Boys' Outing', how did Trigger suggest the Jolly Boys get back to Peckham after they discovered there was a train strike?

....

791 In 'The Yellow Peril', in what Scandinavian capital city did Trigger say the contact he bought the paint from lived?

....

792. In 'May the Force Be with You', what did Trigger point to in an attempt to warn Rodney that Slater was a policeman?

....

793 In 'Homesick', Rodney asked Trigger why he kept calling him by the wrong Christian name. To prove Trigger wrong Rodney mentioned two documents he had with 'Rodney' written on them. Name either document.

....

794 In 'Video Nasty', Rodney told Trigger that he had been commissioned to make a film. What '*dessert*' did Trigger say he would not leave Rodney to make, let alone a film?

....

SERIES 5 – PART 1

795 In 'From Prussia with Love', who did Del Boy tell Anna would investigate him when she decided to keep her baby: The Inland Revenue, Poll Tax Office or HM Customs & Excise?

....

796 In 'The Miracle of Peckham', when Del Boy was being interviewed for television, he named three different awards that he said he didn't want after witnessing the miracle. Name any one of them.

....

797 In 'The Longest Night', name any one of the four employee groups Del Boy told the shoplifter/robber would already be in the store when he decided to make his getaway.

....

798 In 'Tea for Three', what type of car did Del Boy land on top of when he crashed to earth in the hang-glider: Ford Escort, Ford Fiesta or Ford Sierra?

....

799 In 'Video Nasty', what major blockbuster terror movie from the 1970s did Del Boy say his story about the rhinoceros was similar to?

....

800 In 'Who Wants To Be A Millionaire?', what country had Del Boy's mate been living in prior to visiting Peckham again?

....

801 In 'From Prussia With Love', what qualification was the father of Anna's baby celebrating the night he visited her room?

....

802 In 'Tea for Three', what was the name of the major high street electrical store that Del Boy said would probably be seeking payment after he crashed into an outside aerial?

....

803 In 'The Longest Night', Del Boy said that he not only knew the shoplifter/robber's name and address but also his mum's ....
Can you recall the two missing words?

....

804 In 'Video Nasty', when Marlene told Del Boy that Boycie had a '*low count*', what did Rodney ask Boycie if he wanted to buy?

....

MIXED BAG – 11

805 In 'A Slow Bus to Chingford', Del Boy dreamed of being *'the Freddie ..... of the highway'*. What was Freddie's surname?

....

806 In 'A Losing Streak', what did Del Boy offer up as a £1,000 bet in addition to his jewellery and Trigger's car?

....

807 In 'No Greater Love', name either of the two items for which Del Boy said Mrs Singh owed him money.

....

808 In 'The Yellow Peril', when Grandad asked Del Boy if the room he was in was the kitchen of the Chinese takeaway, what bedroom did Del Boy say it was?

....

809 In 'A Touch of Glass', what normally very reliable make of car was her Ladyship driving when the Trotters noticed her stranded at the roadside?

....

810 In 'Friday The 14th', Del Boy gagged the gamekeeper by mistake. What did the police sergeant say the gamekeeper suffered from?

....

811 In 'Hole in One', how many previous lawsuits did we discover Uncle Albert had been involved in: 15, 20 or 25?

....

812 In 'Watching the Girls Go By', after Del Boy pointed out a girl he should chat up in a bar, what saint did Rodney ask Del Boy if he looked like?

....

813 In 'As One Door Closes', what happened to the rare butterfly that Rodney caught at the end of the episode?

....

814 In 'Video Nasty', Del Boy gave Rodney a large list of extras for inclusion in his film. What did Mickey Pearce think the list was when he saw it?

....

'WHO WANTS TO BE A MILLIONAIRE?'

815 At the beginning of the episode we see Boycie entering The Nag's Head with an old friend of Del Boy's. What was his name: Jumbo Cummings, Jumbo Mills or Jumbo Simpkins?

....

816 When Jumbo listened to Uncle Albert playing the piano in the pub, what type of licence did Jumbo tell Uncle Albert The Nag's Head did not have?

....

817 When Del Boy commented on how well Jumbo was looking, Jumbo told him it was because of the weather down under. Apart from frost, what else did Jumbo say you couldn't find in Australia?

....

818 Del Boy and Jumbo used to be business partners during the 1960s. What type of stall did they have?

....

819 What was the bet that Del Boy made with Boycie about Jumbo?

....

820 How much was the above bet for?

....

821 Jumbo told Del Boy that he met with Boycie to secure a deal
     whereby Boycie would supply him with prestige European motors
     for export to Australia. Name either of the two makes of car that
     Jumbo mentioned to Del Boy.

....

822 When Del Boy ordered a bottle of champagne for himself and
     Jumbo in The Nag's Head, whose favourite champagne did Del Boy
     tell Jumbo it was?

....

823 Jumbo asked Del Boy to go into partnership with him in Australia.
     What would Del Boy's role be in their new partnership involving
     cars?

....

824 Why was Rodney refused an immigration visa to enter Australia?

....

'A ROYAL FLUSH'

825 What dining room set was Del Boy flogging in the market at the beginning of the episode?

....

826 Where were the above items made: India, Indonesia or Iraq?

....

827 What did Del Boy tell his customers in the market he was insured for? Sounds like car insurance!

....

828 What was the Christian name of the girl Rodney met in the market and took for lunch: Valerie, Vanessa or Victoria?

....

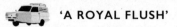

829 What was the girl in No. 828 attempting to sell in the market?

....

830 What did Rodney tell the girl in No. 828 he was a partner in?

....

831 Can you recall where Rodney agreed to take the girl in No. 828 the day after they first met?

....

832 For where did Del Boy get tickets in order that Rodney could impress his new girlfriend?

....

833 Del Boy claimed that if he married his new girlfriend Rodney could one day end up in the House of Lords. What did Uncle Albert say they could then watch Rodney do on television?

....

834 What did Del Boy get Trigger to pretend Del Boy was, when he spotted several policemen and women scouring the marketplace?

....

'THE FROG'S LEGACY'

835 What was Del Boy attempting to sell Mike in The Nag's Head at the beginning of this episode?

....

836 How much did Del Boy say the item in No. 835 would cost in the shops: £299, £399 or £499?

....

837 Trigger thought his beer tasted funny and asked Uncle Albert to sample it. Uncle Albert said it reminded him of the water from a very famous river. Can you name the river?

....

838 When Mike told Trigger that he had received certificates for his beer, what was Trigger's response?

....

839 What item necessary for Del Boy's everyday work did Rodney refer to when he called Del Boy and the item '*The Deadly Duo*'?

....

840 What was the occupation of the man Del Boy was speaking to in The Nag's Head and who complained to Del Boy that a computer he bought from him was destroying all of his business records?

....

841 Trigger informed the boys that his niece was getting married. Can you recall her first name?

....

842 Del Boy managed to get Rodney a job working for the man in No. 840. When Del Boy was telling Rodney about the job he said that the gentleman had mentioned his 'CV'. What did Del Boy think the gentleman had meant by the term CV?

....

843 Del Boy, Rodney and Uncle Albert were all invited to the wedding in No. 841. What did Del Boy buy the happy couple for their wedding?

....

844 When Boycie saw Del Boy's present wrapped up, he said it looked like someone been at it given the poor state it was in. Who was that person?

....

'DATES'

845 At the beginning of the episode, Del Boy and Rodney were in the flat celebrating an excellent month of sales. What ladies' grooming device had they sold more than 400 of in the past four weeks?

....

846 Whose birthday was it in the episode: Del Boy's, Rodney's or Uncle Albert's?

....

847 What was in the box that Uncle Albert carried from the bedroom into the living room to show Del Boy and Rodney?

....

848 How old did Uncle Albert say he was when he first joined the Navy: 16, 17 or 18?

....

849 When Uncle Albert told the boys how he was responsible for crashing into a USS Aircraft Carrier, what singer did Del Boy mention when he said that they would have stood more of a chance if the singer had been in the crow's nest?

....

850 Who walked into The Nag's Head wearing a blue suit and carrying a bunch of flowers for his blind date?

....

851 What was organisation that Boycie informed the boys in The Nag's Head he had just become a member of?

....

852 What type of job did Trigger tell the computer dating agency he did to add a bit of '*glamour*' to his personal file?

....

853 What type of meal did Del Boy inform the computer dating agency employee that the lucky girl on his blind date would be guaranteed?

....

854 What was the Christian name of the girl the computer dating agency arranged for Del Boy to meet?

....

'YUPPY LOVE'

855 What Diploma course did Rodney tell Uncle Albert he was studying for at the beginning of the episode?

....

856 When Rodney was explaining to Del Boy how their flat was only 15 minutes away from the West End and 15 minutes away from the motorway, what was Uncle Albert's '*15-minute*' response?

....

857 When Rodney was 11 years old what type of '*gas*' did he say was being introduced to the Estate?

....

858 When Del Boy pulled up outside the wine bar he noticed two attractive young women get out of a car and enter the bar. What make of car were the girls in?

....

859 When Del Boy was trying to impress the two girls in the wine bar, what type of '*Market*' did he say he worked in?

....

860 What '*type*' of Beaujolais did Del Boy order in the wine bar?

....

861 What made Cassandra first approach Rodney at the evening college?

....

862 Which one of Del Boy's mates entered the wine bar a short time after him?

....

863 What type of pie did Mike accuse Trigger of stealing in The Nag's Head?

....

864 When Del Boy told Rodney that Cassandra had phoned him, he mentioned that she was going out the next day to purchase tickets for a pop concert. What was the name of the group Del Boy said he bet they would be going to see?

....

'DANGER UXD'

865 What was Del Boy's reply when he told Uncle Albert that the video would record all their favourite TV shows when they were on holiday, and Uncle Albert asked him how the video recorder would know that they were on holiday?

....

866 What did Del Boy have boxes upon boxes of in the flat and also crammed into his fridge?

....

867 In The Nag's Head Mike served Denzil a bowl of stew and then served the same dish to a '*yuppy*'. What did he describe the stew as to the yuppy?

....

868 Can you remember the name of Denzil's courier business: Transworld ....?

....

869 What made all of the yuppies start to hang around Peckham and eat and drink in The Nag's Head?

....

870 What type of '*water*' did Denzil say was '*under the bridge*' when he was talking about Del Boy's spat with one of the yuppies?

....

871 When Rodney's suit was stained with tomato juice, Del Boy asked Mike to give him something to clean it up with. What did Mike suggest he should use?

....

872 Do you remember what dangerous substance the dolls Del Boy was attempting to sell were full of?

....

873 How did Del Boy and Rodney manage to get the dolls out of the flat and into the van without raising suspicion?

....

874 What excuse did Uncle Albert give for not being able to drive, when Del Boy asked him to drive the van a few yards to him and Rodney?

....

'CHAIN GANG'

875 What is the name of the club that the boys are in at the beginning of the episode?

....

876 When talking about Rodney and Cassandra to Trigger, what did Del Boy say Rodney had been 'blown out' more times than?

....

877 Can you recall the first name of the retired jeweller that Del Boy was doing business with?

....

878 What make of car was the retired jeweller driving when Del Boy and Rodney met him in the car park of the casino?

....

879 How many gold chains were in the briefcase inspected by Del Boy and Rodney?

....

880 Excluding Del Boy, name four members of the consortium Del Boy pulled together to purchase the consignment of gold chains?

....

881 What type of restaurant did the boys travel to in order that the retired jeweller could meet up with his contact that wanted to buy the gold chains?

....

882 What did the retired jeweller ask the waiter to get him when the waiter asked him what he would like to order?

....

883 Where did Del Boy get put through to when he hit redial on the telephone in the flat hoping that it would be the same number that the retired jeweller had telephoned earlier?

....

884 After Del Boy and his consortium had been set up over the gold chains, another friend of Del Boy's had put a consortium together in similar circumstances? Can you name him?

....

SERIES 3 – PART 2

885 In 'Homesick', Grandad gave Rodney something that had been left to Grandad by his Grandad. What did he give Rodney?

....

886 In 'Healthy Competition', Del Boy told Rodney that business was poor, but good if you compared it to what type of gin salesman?

....

887 In 'Friday The 14th', which one of the utility cards in a game of Monopoly did Grandad own?

....

888 In 'Yesterday Never Comes', what did Del Boy give Miranda as a birthday present?

....

889 In 'May the Force Be with You', what did Del Boy ask Slater for in return for giving Slater the name of the person who stole the microwave oven?

....

890 In 'Wanted', what did Del Boy offer Rodney in place of chicken after Rodney made the sound of a cat in the tank room?

....

891 In 'Healthy Competition', what did Del Boy buy as a special treat for Grandad: strawberries, ice cream or toffee?

....

892 In 'Friday The 14th', how many different counties' police forces were searching for the Mad Axe Killer?

....

893 In 'Yesterday Never Comes', did Miranda refer to Del Boy's Gran as Mrs Char, Mrs Mop or Mrs Shine?

....

894 In 'May the Force Be with You', what household heating item did Del Boy remind the constable that he sold to his mother?

....

895 In 'As One Door Closes', where was Denzil going when he met Del Boy and Rodney in the market?

....

896 In 'Hole in One', Del Boy commented that his jewellery knew more about '*hock*' than a wine taster from a particular country. What country did Del Boy mention?

....

897 In 'Sleeping Dogs Lie', when Uncle Albert was being discharged from hospital, what did Del Boy tell Rodney to keep a close eye on when Uncle Albert was passing them?

....

898 In 'Watching the Girls Go By', when Uncle Albert saw Rodney in the flat dressed from top to bottom in black and white, what type of hat did he tell Rodney would look good on him?

....

899 In 'As One Door Closes', what was the consignment of louvre doors going to be used for?

....

900 In 'Happy Returns', why was Junie's husband sent to prison?

....

901 In 'Strained Relations', name either of the two things that Uncle Albert said had been built in place of the seaman's mission?

....

902 In 'Hole in One', the judge asked Del Boy how suffering from amnesia made Uncle Albert continually fall down. What was Del Boy's explanation?

....

903 In 'Watching the Girls Go By', what was the name of the *high-scoring* actress that Del Boy said Rodney had no chance of finding a look-a-like of in Peckham?

....

904 In 'As One Door Closes', what was the rare butterfly sitting on when Rodney caught it?

....

SERIES 5 – PART 2

905 In 'From Prussia With Love', what part of his body did Del Boy tell Rodney to take out of Dukie's mouth when they visited Boycie and Marlene's home?

....

906 In 'The Longest Night', where was the shoplifter's toy gun made: Taiwan, Indonesia or South Korea?

....

907 In 'Tea For Three', what '*Board*' did Del Boy say had narrowly beaten The Nag's Head in a beer contest?

....

908 In 'Video Nasty', when Uncle Albert asked Del Boy why the rhinoceros in his story killed people, what type of '*worker*' did Del Boy ask Uncle Albert if he thought it should be instead?

....

909 In 'Who Wants To Be A Millionaire?' what slang word did Del Boy give to the wig Jumbo was wearing?

....

910 In 'Video Nasty', what excuse did Mickey give Rodney as an explanation as to why she was wearing a nurse's uniform when he brought her to the Trotters' flat?

....

911 In 'The Longest Night', name any one of the two luxury health items the manager of the supermarket's wife had installed at their home.

....

912 In 'Tea For Three', what did Del Boy say he was prepared to '*throw in for free*' along with the home solarium he was trying to sell to Mike at The Nag's Head?

....

913 In 'Video Nasty', Del Boy signed up so many extras for Rodney's film that Rodney commented that he had more extras than there were in a famous multi-Oscar-winning movie. What famous movie did Rodney mention?

....

914 In 'Who Wants To Be A Millionaire?', what was the only thing, belonging to Mike, that Jumbo claimed was working?

....

MIXED BAG – 12

915 In 'The Russians are Coming', where did Del Boy borrow the Portaloo from?

....

916 In 'No Greater Love', why did Irene end her relationship with Rodney?

....

917 In 'The Yellow Peril', why was Mr Chin so anxious to have the kitchen at his Chinese takeaway painted?

....

918 In 'Diamonds are for Heather', what did Del Boy order a bottle of in the Indian restaurant?

....

919 In 'Happy Returns', what did Del Boy tell Debbie he would buy her for her birthday?

....

920 In 'Sleeping Dogs Lie', what did Del Boy ask Rodney whether he had accidentally done to Dukie when he was putting him in the van?

....

921 In 'Watching the Girls Go By', what shop did the girl that both Mickey Pearce and Uncle Albert asked Rodney if he was taking to the party evening at The Nag's Head work?

....

922 In 'As One Door Closes', what was the first thing the boys used in an attempt to capture the rare butterfly?

....

923 In 'Tea For Three', what did Rodney say made his face hurt when he did it?

....

924 In 'Video Nasty', what famous American Hollywood actor did Del Boy say was similar to the private detective character in the story he had in mind for Rodney's film: Charles Bronson, Kirk Douglas or Charlton Heston?

....

'THE UNLUCKY WINNER IS...'

925 Can you complete the title of Rodney's painting – *Marble Arch at* ......

....

926 What French Historic Monument was Rodney's painting originally depicting?

....

927 '*Captain* ....'. Can you complete the name Del Boy referred to Uncle Albert as? (Clue: Frozen Food)

....

928 What '*car*' magazine was Rodney reading in The Nag's Head?

....

929 What was the name of the cornflake company that gave Rodney first prize in a painting competition?

....

930 To where in Spain did Rodney win a holiday?

....

931 Name any one of the three different items Rodney purchased in the chemist's because he was too embarrassed to ask for a packet of condoms.

....

932 What was the name of the gang that Rodney was made an honorary member of?

....

933 What tickets did Del Boy purchase for himself, Cassandra and Rodney?

....

934 What '*Finals*' was Rodney in at the disco?

....

'SICKNESS AND WEALTH'

935 What '*robotic*' character from a 1970s' TV show did Rodney describe as jumping around like Uncle Albert's spin dryer?

....

936 What did Uncle Albert present Rodney with for his tea at the beginning of the episode: a fry-up, a Chinese or pizza & chips?

....

937 What was the name of the Scottish doctor that Del Boy was very friendly with?

....

938 What drink did Del Boy mix into his Andrews Liver Salts for his sore stomach?

....

939 What did Uncle Albert say Elsie Partridge was when he was talking to Del Boy about the supernatural?

....

940 What did Del Boy book a room for at The Nag's Head that involved Elsie Partridge?

....

941 When three loud bumps were heard on the ceiling at The Nag's Head, Del Boy said that the noise either meant Elsie Partridge was ready to start or else she had cramp... in what?

....

942 What was the name of the barmaid at The Nag's Head who Rodney took out on a date?

....

943 What city in India did Del Boy's doctor say she was from?

....

944 What was Del Boy diagnosed as suffering from when he was in hospital?

....

'LITTLE PROBLEMS'

945 Why was Rodney so despondent at the beginning of the episode when he was sitting at a table in The Nag's Head?

....

946 Who offered Rodney a job?

....

947 What was the latest '*Executive*' bargain that Del Boy was selling in this episode?

....

948 What initials did Del Boy have placed after Rodney's name when he had headed notepaper printed for *Trotters' Independent Traders*?

....

949 What were Boycie and Trigger watching on TV in The Nag's Head?

....

950 Can you name either of the two people that Del Boy took 200 mobile phones from on a '*sale or return*' basis?

....

951 What was the surname of the brothers who Boycie said were looking for Del Boy?

....

952 When the comedian at Rodney's stag night was making fun of Uncle Albert, Uncle Albert told him that he had fought in the war. What war did the comedian mention?

....

953 Can you name the Simply Red song that was playing at Rodney's wedding reception?

....

954 What did Rodney do at the end of the episode that indicated he had forgotten he was married?

....

955 In 'Danger UXD', what was Del Boy's response when Uncle Albert asked him whether he wanted any breakfast?

....

956 In 'Chain Gang', when Rodney said he had a tickle in his throat, what did Del Boy say was probably stuck in it after he witnessed him kissing Cassandra?

....

957 In 'The Unlucky Winner Is…', when Cassandra told Del Boy that Rodney's art teacher thought his painting *Marble Arch at Dawn* was a masterpiece, what did Del Boy say the art teacher actually called it?

....

958 In 'Sickness and Wealth', what did Del Boy say the steam from
     Uncle Albert's spin dryer was doing to the kitchen units?

....

959 In 'Yuppy Love', what did Del Boy tell Rodney they would be
     calling in a minute when Rodney was standing on the steps of
     the Adult Education Centre?

....

960 In 'Chain Gang', what did Del Boy say Arnie had suffered when he
     was in the Italian restaurant?

....

961 In 'Sickness and Wealth', what cockney slang word for '*pain*'
     did Del Boy use when he visited his doctor?

....

962 In 'Danger UXD', Del Boy said three things gave him his yuppy
     image – his aluminium briefcase, his Filofax and a car key ring.
     What type of car was the key ring for?

....

963 In 'Yuppy Love', what '*TV information character*' did Del Boy
     tell Rodney to remember what he had said when he was crossing
     the road?

....

964 In 'The Unlucky Winner Is…', what was the name of the disco
     Rodney had to go to with the other children who were also
     competition prize winners?

....

'THE JOLLY BOYS' OUTING'

965 What was Del Boy trying to sell in the market at the beginning of the episode?

....

966 What seaside resort were the boys off to for their Jolly Boys' Outing?

....

967 What department of Cassandra's father's business was Rodney the head of?

....

968 What continent did Cassandra's boss mention when he was telling Del Boy and Cassandra's father that it was worth investing in?

....

969 When Cassandra's boss said he had spent some time recently in *Afrique-sur-Mer*, what was Del Boy's '*foreign-speak*' reply?

....

970 What was the American ball game that Cassandra's boss said he had to get up early the next morning to play?

....

971 What popular board game did the dinner party guests play in Cassandra and Rodney's flat?

....

972 What famous comic title did Del Boy describe the Jolly Boys' Outing as?

....

973 Name any of the two boys who were playing football in the car park at the halfway house.

....

974 What was the name of the B B that Del Boy, Rodney and Uncle Albert stayed in?

....

'RODNEY COME HOME'

975 What did Del Boy tell Uncle Albert to get the both of them for lunch at the start of the episode when they were in the shopping centre?

....

976 Who did Rodney see passing by his office when he was looking out of the window?

....

977 Name any of the three '*Naval terms*' that Del Boy told Uncle Albert to call out if he saw a security guard approaching them at the shopping centre.

....

978 Speaking to Racquel about Del Boy, what 'vow' did Rodney say Del Boy took when he joined a monastery?

....

979 What did Racquel tell Del Boy she was afraid of when she was lying alone in bed?

....

980 What was Rodney doing when his secretary brought a client into his office for a meeting?

....

981 What sport did Cassandra say she was going out to play when Rodney arrived back at their apartment?

....

982 What happened to Uncle Albert's beard when Del Boy was preparing the dinner table for the meal he was having with Racquel?

....

983 What type of pub sports' team did Del Boy claim the girl Rodney was planning to take to the cinema once lived with?

....

984 What word beginning with the letter 'D' did Del Boy describe women as that offended Racquel when he said he saw a programme on TV about AIDS?

....

985 Where did Uncle Albert think Racquel slept at the flat?

....

986 Uncle Albert made himself some eggs and bacon for breakfast but what was sitting on the table ready for Del Boy to eat?

....

987 Name either of the two papers that uncle Albert presented Del Boy with at the beginning of the episode when Del Boy was sitting down for breakfast.

....

988 What make of car did Del Boy say Uncle Albert's laugh sounded like?

....

989 What excuse did Rodney give Uncle Albert as being wrong with him when he asked him to call work on his behalf and say he was sick?

....

990 What '*slang term*' did Del Boy refer to the Hoover as when he asked Racquel to switch it off in the flat?

....

991 Instead of Cassandra's plane landing in London, to what northwest airport was it re-routed by Air Traffic Control?

....

992 Can you recall the '*cowboy*' name Del Boy called Marlene's brother when he saw him at Boycie's house?

....

993 When Cassandra was looking through Del Boy's old address book, what did Del Boy have besides some of the girls' names in his book?

....

994 From which London airport was the radar transmitter dish that Del Boy bought believing it was a satellite dish stolen?

....

995 At the beginning of the episode what was on the tray that Del Boy was carrying along with three cups of tea: croissants, jam biscuits or toast?

....

996 What accidentally happened to one of the cups of tea on the tray that Del Boy was carrying?

....

997 What did Del Boy say he and Racquel were going to be doing at the flat that prompted Rodney to want to change his mind about meeting up with Cassandra?

....

998 What was the latest '*musical device*' that Del Boy was attempting to sell?

....

999   When Marlene asked Del Boy if he had missed Rodney after
      their partnership had broken up, what was Del Boy's response?
      (Clue: 'Wake Me Up Before You Go Go'.)

....

1000 How did Del Boy arrange for Cassandra and Rodney to meet
      up again after they had split up?

....

1001 Who did Del Boy not want Racquel to meet when Rodney told
      him that she was on her way to The Nag's Head?

....

1002 Can you recall the name of the set designer that Racquel's agent
      introduced him to: Jeremy, Jules or Julian?

....

1003 What did Rodney do following some advice he received from
      Uncle Albert about an officer who was on his boat and who
      avoided a court marshall?

....

1004 What news did Del Boy have for Rodney and Uncle Albert that
      made him waken the two boys at the end of the episode?

....

'STAGE FRIGHT'

1005   What according to Rodney had the local magistrates' court given Del Boy because he had appeared there so often?

....

1006   How did Del Boy refer to the baby that Racquel was carrying that put Rodney off the sandwich he was eating?

....

1007   What government agency/department did Del Boy say he never actually got around to registering *Trotters' Independent Traders* as an official business with?

....

1008   Excluding clothing, name any two of the four props Tony used in his act?

....

1009 What letter of the alphabet did Tony the singer say he could not pronounce properly?

....

1010 Can you recall the name of the '*music business*' that Del Boy set up: The T......... I........... S......... A........... ?

....

1011 What did Boycie say the owner of the nightclub nailed the nightclub manager to every time he didn't like the cabaret act that he'd booked?

....

1012 What was the first song that Racquel and Tony sang at the nightclub?

....

1013 For what did Uncle Albert take money from Del Boy that led Del Boy to accuse Uncle Albert of cheating him?

....

1014 What did Del Boy shout to Tony from the flat of the balcony at the end of the episode?

....

'THE CLASS OF '62'

1015 Where was 'The Class of '62' reunion held?

....

1016 Who booked the venue and organised 'The Class of '62' reunion?

....

1017 What is the latest '*business machine*' that Del Boy is attempting to sell?

....

1018 Apart from Roy Slater and Del Boy, can you name four of the other five people who attended 'The Class of '62' reunion?

....

1019 At school Del Boy said he used to play like Paul Gascoigne. What '*Gascoigne*' did Del Boy say Boycie used to play football like?

....

1020 What '*term of friendship*' used by Del Boy did Trigger mistake for the name of an Italian boy at school?

....

1021 What Christian name, also beginning with the letter 'R', did Roy Slater call Racquel that confused Uncle Albert?

....

1022 When Del Boy told Rodney that he was in a state of shock, Rodney likened it to being hit by a free kick from an ex-Watford, Liverpool and England player. Can you name the footballer concerned?

....

1023 What was the drink that Slater said Del Boy should always buy him at The Nag's Head to prevent him from getting drunk and letting everyone know that he was Racquel's estranged husband?

....

1024 What was it that Slater had stolen, and needed a divorce from Racquel for, so that she would have no claim to the items?

....

'HE AIN'T HEAVY, HE'S MY UNCLE'

1025 When Del Boy saw Uncle Albert in his vest and shorts exercising in the flat, what famous footballer's name did he call him by?

....

1026 When Del Boy saw Rodney first thing in the morning, what cult horror movie did he say Rodney reminded him was playing in the nearby cinema?

....

1027 What game were Uncle Albert and another gentleman playing in The Nag's Head?

....

1028 What did Rodney tell Del Boy had happened to Uncle Albert on his way home from The Nag's Head?

....

1029 Can you recall the film starring Robert Redford that Racquel reminded Del Boy was just about to come on TV?

....

1030 Why did Uncle Albert let out a cry when he was sitting on the armchair in the flat?

....

1031 What make and model of car did Boycie sell Del Boy?

....

1032 Can you recall the name of the '*Road*' Uncle Albert visited to remind him of growing up as a boy? (Clue: smoking)

....

1033 What occupation were the skinheads that Del Boy thought were thugs and who had been drinking in The Nag's Head over the past couple of weeks?

....

1034 What sport did Uncle Albert claim he was a champion of when he was in the Royal Navy?

....

'THREE MEN, A WOMAN AND A BABY'

1035 What Chinese takeaway meal were there still some leftovers of sitting on the table in the flat at the beginning of the episode?

....

1036 What did Uncle Albert tell Rodney that Del Boy and Racquel were thinking of calling their baby?

....

1037 What was Del Boy's latest money-making '*item*' that he was selling in this episode?

....

1038 Which one of Rodney's mates did he tell Del Boy had recently become a vegetarian?

....

1039 When Rodney was talking to Del Boy about '*Green Issues*', what famous environmentalist musician did Del Boy refer to Rodney as?

....

1040 Who did Del Boy say was in borstal the last time Uncle Albert '*got his leg over*'?

....

1041 What happened when the male midwife bent over to examine Racquel when she was in labour?

....

1042 What did Rodney ask Del Boy if there were any of when Del Boy told him that he could see the baby's head?

....

1043 What did Del Boy and Racquel call their baby boy?

....

1044 Which of Del Boy's most-famous lines did he speak to his son when we saw Del Boy standing holding him at the end of the episode?

....

SERIES 7 – PART 1

1045 In 'The Sky's The Limit', what occupation did Racquel say her estranged husband was?

....

1046 In 'The Chance of a Lunchtime', what was the name of Del Boy's ex-fiancée that he met again in The Nag's Head: Tanya, Tracey or Trudy?

....

1047 In 'Stage Fright', what did Del Boy say turned up when General Custer was least expecting it?

....

1048 In 'The Class of '62', what famous female British singer did Del Boy imply he knew personally when he was in a nightclub where Racquel had an audition?

....

1049 In 'He Ain't Heavy, He's My Uncle', what was the name that Rodney used to describe Del Boy's Ford Capri Ghia?

....

1050 In 'Three Men, A Woman and A Baby', what city's stock exchange did Uncle Albert say was just opening as the New York stock exchange was closing?

....

1051 In 'The Sky's The Limit', can you recall either of the two terms Uncle Albert used when he phoned in sick on Rodney's behalf?

....

1052 In 'The Chance of a Lunchtime' what country's National Anthem was heard playing when Rodney rang the doorbell at the flat that Del Boy saluted to?

....

1053 In 'Stage Fright', which one of Del Boy's mates did Tony the Singer work with?

....

1054 In 'The Class of '62', who sent Del Boy his first fax message?

....

SERIES 6 – PART 2

1055 In 'Yuppy Love', where were the tomatoes that Del Boy was selling from?

....

1056 In 'Danger UXD', what '*Overture*' was Uncle Albert humming on his way into the kitchen near the beginning of the episode?

....

1057 In 'Chain Gang', what happened to Mike's car outside the restaurant?

....

1058 In 'The Unlucky Winner Is…', what was Del Boy's reasoning behind posting his entries for competitions a couple of days before the closing date?

....

1059 In 'Sickness and Wealth', what *Star Wars* character did Rodney tell Uncle Albert reminded him of his spin dryer break-dancing?

....

1060 In 'Little Problems', what did Rodney forget to take account of that caused his unmanned space probe in his examination to fall short of its final destination?

....

1061 In 'Yuppy Love', how did Del Boy end up falling to the floor in the wine bar?

....

1062 In 'Danger UXD', how did the owner of the Advanced Electronics Research and Development Centre acquire the Queen's Award for Industry?

....

1063 In 'Chain Gang', what did Arnie say he had not paid on the gold chains, thereby allowing him to sell them to Del Boy at a cheap price?

....

1064 In 'The Unlucky Winner Is…', what did Del Boy tell Cassandra to '*get sorted out*' prior to them going on holiday?

....

MIXED BAG – 13

1065 In 'No Greater Love', what '*Hall*' did Irene tell Rodney her son was at?

....

1066 In 'The Yellow Peril', what else did Mr Chin want the Trotters to paint after they painted his kitchen?

....

1067 In 'Friday The 14th', how many years had the Mad Axe Killer spent at the institute before escaping?

....

1068 In 'Happy Returns', Del Boy persuaded Rodney to leave Debbie's home early one evening. Who did Del Boy say he had seen on the estate that frightened Rodney?

....

1069 In 'Strained Relations', Uncle Albert asked Rodney if he knew
what nickname he had been given in the Navy. Upon hearing the
number of times his ships had been torpedoed, what nickname
did Rodney offer?

....

1070 In 'Watching the Girls Go By', how did Del Boy imply Helga lost
the little finger from her right hand?

....

1071 In 'As One Door Closes', what was covering the grave where
Del Boy pointed, stating that Rodney would be buried there?

....

1072 In 'To Hull and Back', how did the boys manage to find their
way back to Hull?

....

1073 In 'The Longest Night', Del Boy referred to the Head of Security
as '*Dixon of* ....'. Can you complete the two missing
words?

....

1074 In 'Video Nasty', what type of '*balls*' did Boycie order at the
Chinese takeaway?

....

1075 Why were Del Boy, Racquel, Rodney, Uncle Albert and friends of The Trotter Clan inside a church at the beginning of the episode?

....

1076 When Mickey was taking the group photo outside the church he set the camera to auto-timer. What did he place the camera on top of?

....

1077 What was Del Boy's latest money-making idea in this episode?

....

1078 Apart from Del Boy and Rodney, who else was going to Florida for their holidays?

....

1079 By what term did Del Boy refer to Rodney's pension money?

....

1080 Why could Cassandra not go to Miami with Rodney?

....

1081 How did Racquel overhear Del Boy speaking to Uncle Albert
about how he would persuade Racquel to allow him to go to
Miami with Rodney?

....

1082 When Uncle Albert suggested that Rodney should take Mickey
Pearce to Miami with him, why did Del Boy say Mickey could
not go?

....

1083 What did Racquel ask Del Boy to bring her into the bedroom
towards the end of the episode?

....

1084 Who did Del Boy bump into in the airport queue at the end of
the episode, which led Del Boy to turn round and say to Rodney
that anyone would think the man owned the plane?

....

1085　What was the full christening name of Del Boy's and Racquel's baby?

....

1086　What Book of the Bible was Del Boy referring to when he said that God knew a bit of '*bunce*' when he saw it?

....

1087　From what country was the Riesling wine that Del Boy purchased a consignment of?

....

1088　Name the '*Holy*' City Del Boy mentioned when speaking to the Vicar after the christening?

....

1089 Rodney shared the same room at Del Boy's flat that Damien slept in. When Rodney was lying in bed one night we saw Damien standing in his cot staring at him. What famous movie theme did we hear being played?

....

1090 What mother from the series purchased the baby intercom set for Del Boy and Racquel?

....

1091 When Uncle Albert asked Del Boy if he could persuade Racquel to allow him to travel to Miami with Rodney, Del Boy's response was 'Can F.... ski?' What name did he mention?

....

1092 When Del Boy invited Rodney into the 'Executive Boardroom' to talk to him about Miami, into what room did Del Boy take Rodney?

....

1093 What type of swimming trunks did Del Boy pack for his trip to Miami?

....

1094 At the end of the episode, Del Boy said that the sooner they got on the plane the sooner ..... could take off. What is the missing word?

....

1095   With what airline did Del Boy and Rodney fly to the United States of America?

....

1096   What did Del Boy hire out for him and Rodney to stay in when they were in Miami?

....

1097   What was the main reason Del Boy gave Rodney for wanting to go into the nightclub in Miami?

....

1098   What was the surname of the '*Don's*' mansion where Del Boy and Rodney stayed?

....

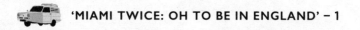

1099 What nationality did a number of different people that Del Boy and Rodney met in Miami think they were?

....

1100 When Del Boy and Rodney took a sightseeing cruise, can you name the pop star that Del Boy called out to when he saw him standing on his lawn?

....

1101 From what country were the drug barons that visited the mansion where Del Boy and Rodney stayed?

....

1102 What excuse was given by the family as the reason why the phone lines in the mansion they were staying in were not working?

....

1103 When Uncle Albert saw Racquel burdened down with shopping bags, he asked her where she had been. Racquel's response included the name of a horseracing course. Can you name it?

....

1104 Describe the shape of cocktail cabinet in the Don's office.

....

'MIAMI TWICE: OH TO BE IN ENGLAND' – 2

1105 When Del Boy was on the flight to Miami did he tell Rodney that they had joined the Glitterati, Mile High Club or the Millionaires' Club?

....

1106 What did Rodney tell Del Boy that he did not even want to see one hanging from their car aerial when they were in Miami?

....

1107 What happened when Del Boy and Rodney stopped their taxi from the airport to ask a young boy to take their photograph with the Miami skyline in the background?

....

1108 Rodney told Del Boy that he would sleep in the camper van with Del Boy on the condition that Del Boy did not eat a particular dish during their stay. Name the dish.

....

1109 What song about '*Texas*' was Del Boy singing while driving on the wrong side of the road in Miami?

....

1110 What reason did Don Occhetti's lawyer give the Don for not being able to prove that he was innocent of all charges brought against him?

....

1111 What did Del Boy do with the wine bottle cork when the owner of the restaurant handed it to him to test the bouquet?

....

1112 What was the nickname of the bodyguard, beginning with the letter 'L', who lent Rodney some of his clothes?

....

1113 What word beginning with the letter 'N' did Rodney use when he asked Del Boy if he thought the Don's son was gay?

....

1114 What was the footballer's name that Del Boy used twice when he greeted the owner of the restaurant?

....

'MOTHER NATURE'S SON' – 1

1115 There is a dream sequence at the beginning of the episode. What Christmas song by Slade do we hear playing?

....

1116 When Racquel asked Uncle Albert if he could remember when he had teeth, what was Rodney's quick response, indicating that Uncle Albert could not remember the last time he had ......?

....

1117 What was the name of Rodney's friend who owned the Garden & Organic Food Centre: Giles, Myles or Styles?

....

1118 What did Del Boy use to place the sample of water in so as it could be taken away and be tested for its purity?

....

1119 Name the two people who Del Boy hired to remove and dump the waste chemicals from his allotment?

....

1120 What was the name of the water that Del Boy bottled and sold?

....

1121 Who at the bank approved Del Boy's loan to get the equipment he needed to run his bottled water business?

....

1122 What English seaside resort town did the Trotters go to for the weekend?

....

1123 Can you recall the name of the famous hotel that the Trotters stayed in?

....

1124 When Del Boy switched the hotel room light off at the end of the episode, what happened to the bottle of water on the bedside table?

....

'MOTHER NATURE'S SON' – 2

1125 What famous British comedian did Rodney say Del Boy reminded him of running around on ecstasy?

....

1126. When Del Boy and his friends were clearing the barrels of waste chemicals from the allotment, what did Del Boy come out of the shed wearing for protection?

....

1127 Where was Del Boy's production factory for his bottled water business?

....

1128 When Rodney told Del Boy that they could be done under the Trade Descriptions Act for calling the water Peckham Spring, what did Del Boy say Sainsbury's sold but didn't come from France?

....

1129 When Del Boy asked Rodney if he thought the Queen would give him an award for his bottled water, what did Rodney imply he was more likely to receive?

....

1130 What famous BBC TV gardener did Mike say he did not see Del Boy as being similar to?

....

1131 What did Del Boy tell Boycie that he needed for his bottled water business to help him distribute the product much quicker?

....

1132 Cassandra and Rodney were booked into the Ambassador Suite at the hotel. What suite were Del Boy, Racquel and Damien booked into?

....

1133 When Damien was lying sleeping in the hotel room Del Boy whisper that when he was a boy, he got an orange and a clip round the what for Christmas?

....

1134 What happened to the London Borough of Peckham as a result of Del Boy's bottled water business?

....

'FATAL EXTRACTION' – 1

1135 What type of 'civil unrest' did we learn was happening in Peckham during this episode from the newspaper that Uncle Albert was reading?

....

1136 What did Racquel ask Uncle Albert to stop boiling on the cooker?

....

1137 What part of Del Boy's body was giving him trouble?

....

1138 What was the latest '*home entertainment*' device that Del Boy was selling in this episode?

....

1139 What did Del Boy decide that Damien was too big for and decide to sell?

....

1140 What type of pet did Del Boy buy Damien?

....

1141 Where did the lady that Del Boy invited out on a date work when he met her at her there?

....

1142 Which one of Del Boy's mates thought he was being called a moron when Del Boy visited the lady he asked out on a date at her place of work?

....

1143 What did Racquel buy Del Boy for Christmas that backfired on Del Boy when played in front of the entire family?

....

1144 What '*Christmas carol*' did we hear being sung at the very end of the episode?

....

'FATAL EXTRACTION' – 2

1145 Name any two of the three things that were on the plates Racquel slammed down on the table at the beginning of the episode.

....

1146 Where did Mickey Pearce meet Rodney when Rodney was on his way over to Del Boy's flat at the beginning of the episode?

....

1147 What type of '*holiday wear*' was Del Boy selling in the market in this episode?

....

1148 Where did Racquel and Damien stay when they left Del Boy?

....

1149 What did Del Boy order with the lemonade when Trigger offered to purchase him a drink in The Nag's Head?

....

1150 What type of biscuit did Del Boy tell Racquel to purchase a hundredweight of for him?

....

1151 What did Del Boy order in The Nag's Head to celebrate the good news that Racquel and Damien had agreed to come back home and live with him?

....

1152 What did Del Boy do in the forecourt of Nelson Mandela House that led to a full-scale riot?

....

1153 What type of hospital did the lady that Del Boy invited out on a date use to work in as a receptionist?

....

1154 What did Racquel throw at Del Boy at the end of the episode?

....

FEATURE-LENGTH SPECIALS – 1

1155 In 'To Hull and Back', what type of '*Pop Rat*' did Del Boy describe Rodney as because of the way he dressed and looked?

....

1156 In 'Strangers on the Shore', can you recall the name of the '*Association*' that sent Uncle Albert a letter?

....

1157 In 'The Frog's Legacy', when Trigger asked Uncle Albert to taste his beer, what country did Uncle Albert say it reminded him of?

....

1158 In 'Miami Twice – The American Dream', what famous '*Movie Cannibal*' did Del Boy say Marlene would scare when she got out of bed first thing in the morning?

....

1159 In 'To Hull and Back', Del Boy nicked two of the diamonds. What did he put in the jewellery bag in place of them?

....

1160 In 'A Royal Flush', was Vicky's Dad the Duke of Marlborough, Mowbray or Marley?

....

1161 In 'Miami Twice: Oh To Be In England', name any one of the three charges the Don was going to be tried for.

....

1162 In 'The Frog's Legacy', what was Del Boy attempting to sell Mike to streamline his business records at The Nag's Head?

....

1163 In 'To Hull and Back', what did Del Boy do with the £15,000 Boycie gave him when he, Rodney and Uncle Albert returned to the flat at the end of the episode?

....

1164 In 'Dates', when Boycie discovered Marlene's dog in his aquarium, what type of fish did Boycie threaten to put in the aquarium to stop the dog from doing it again?

....

MIXED BAG – 14

1165 In 'Rodney Come Home', name any of the two names with alcoholic references that Del Boy said were Rodney's friends: ….. Walker and ….. Bacardi.

....

1166 In 'Yuppy Love', what type of car did Del Boy ask Rodney if Cassandra had, given that she gave him a lift home and he was soaking wet?

....

1167 In 'Miami Twice: The American Dream', what famous make of '*Dinner Set*' did Del Boy say Rodney nearly dropped once when the Vicar handed Damien to Rodney?

....

1168 In 'Watching the Girls Go By', what reptile did the girl who Rodney took to the party evening at The Nag's Head, bring to the pub with her?

....

1169 In 'From Prussia With Love', what did Rodney tell Anna people
      in Peckham would chop her head off for if they knew she had
      some of them in her mouth?

....

1170 In 'The Longest Night', what item of shopping did Del Boy say the
      shoplifter could use as a truncheon when he took up his new job
      with the supermarket?

....

1171 In 'Tea For Three', what did Del Boy say the children called him
      as he flew overhead in the hang-glider?

....

1172 In 'Who Wants To Be A Millionaire?' name any two of the four
      things that Rodney thought Del Boy would need him to do when
      the new cars arrived in Australia.

....

1173 In 'To Hull and Back', what type of spawn did Slater say Del Boy
      put in his milk at school?

....

1174 In 'Sickness and Wealth', Mike claimed that Del Boy had drunk
      more cocktails in the past month than a famous movie spy.
      Who was Mike referring to?

....

SERIES 7 – PART 2

1175 In 'The Sky's The Limit', what former President of the United States' wife did Del Boy mention when he said going on a pub crawl with Alan was like going on one with her?

....

1176 In 'The Chance of a Lunchtime', at what age did Del Boy first say he would be a millionaire when he reached that age?

....

1177 In 'Stage Fright', name either of the two people we could see Racquel standing and talking to at the bar in The Nag's Head.

....

1178 In 'The Class of '62', what was stamped across the boxes containing the fax machines?

....

1179 In 'He Ain't Heavy, He's My Uncle', Del Boy said that Uncle Albert not being interested in women was like a squirrel not being interested in …. What did he say?

....

1180 In 'Three Men, A Woman & A Baby', what '*Baby Competition*' was Mike holding at The Nag's Head?

....

1181 In 'The Sky's The Limit', from who did Boycie purchase his state-of-the-art satellite dish?

....

1182 In 'Stage Fright', what did '*LDA*' stand for when Rodney went to view a flat?

....

1183 In 'The Chance of a Lunchtime', what did Rodney ask Cassandra to show him from her holiday?

....

1184 In 'He Ain't Heavy, He's My Uncle', what colour was Del Boy's Ford Capri Ghia?

....

'HEROES AND VILLAINS' – 1

1185 During Rodney's nightmare at the beginning of the episode, can you name any one of the three products belonging to Del Boy's business empire that we saw being advertised?

....

1186 What did Damien bounce off Rodney's head when Rodney was sitting reading a newspaper in the flat?

....

1187 What happened to Cassandra's specimen urine sample that Rodney had placed in the fridge at the flat?

....

1188 Who did Rodney first suggest to telephone when the van broke down on the way to the fancy dress party?

....

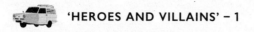

1189 What did Del Boy and Rodney go to the fancy dress party dressed as?

....

1190 How did Del Boy manage to knock the mugger out?

....

1191 What British sprinter did Del Boy liken Rodney to when he said Rodney was running away from the mugger?

....

1192 What way did the local newspapers spell Rodney's name?

....

1193 What good news did Cassandra and Rodney have for Del Boy and Racquel at the end of the episode?

....

1194 For what reason did Del Boy receive a cheque from the local council?

....

'HEROES AND VILLAINS' – 2

1195 During Rodney's nightmare at the beginning of the episode, what was written beneath the large portrait of Del Boy: '….. *Trotter of Peckham.*'

....

1196 What pet did Rodney purchase Cassandra to keep her company at the flat?

....

1197 What type of clocks was Del Boy attempting to sell in this episode?

....

1198 What did Del Boy buy Rodney for his birthday?

....

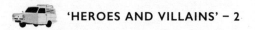

1199 Why did Trigger say the council gave him a silver medal for?

....

1200 What stupid thing was Del Boy doing when he and Rodney lifted the hood of the van and were inspecting the engine area to find out what why it had broken down?

....

1201 When Del Boy said that Boycie had come to the fancy dress party as The Penguin from Batman, what Batman character did Boycie say he was more like?

....

1202 Who appeared dressed as a chauffeur at the fancy dress party?

....

1203 What trendy fashion item, worn on the head, was Del Boy selling in the market?

....

1204 What award did the local council give Del Boy for catching the mugger?

....

'MODERN MEN' – 1

1205 What '*Forest*' did Rodney tell Uncle Albert his beard reminded him of?

....

1206 Name the title of the book Del Boy told Rodney he was reading?

....

1207 What type of coat did Del Boy buy Racquel?

....

1208 Can you recall what operation Del Boy said he was going to have?

....

1209 What belonging to Rodney did Del Boy place an advertisement in the local newspaper for?

....

1210   When Del Boy was talking to Rodney about a sperm bank,
       Rodney misunderstood him. Can you recall the name of the
       high street bank Rodney thought Del Boy was talking about?

       ....

1211   What was the name of the Indian doctor that Del Boy visited?

       ....

1212   As what did Del Boy disguise the horse-riding helmets he
       was selling?

       ....

1213   What did Del Boy do after lecturing Rodney about being strong
       for Cassandra when they were both standing outside the hospital
       room she was in?

       ....

1214   What did Del Boy do to the loud-mouthed man who was abusing
       the hospital reception staff?

       ....

'MODERN MEN' – 2

1215 At the beginning of the episode we see Uncle Albert emerging from the kitchen at the flat with a bowl. What was in the bowl?

....

1216 What colour were the new silk pyjamas Del Boy bought himself?

....

1217 What day of the year did Del Boy say Rodney would close on if he had a flower shop?

....

1218 Rodney told Cassandra that Del Boy thought that sex under a barrow meant '*Market* ....'. What's the missing word?

....

1219 When Rodney told Uncle Albert that he was good with computers, what was Uncle Albert's response?

....

1220 When Rodney was placed on hold while using the phone at the flat, what song loved by Del Boy could we hear playing in the background?

....

1221 What term did Del Boy use when speaking about his sperm cells?

....

1222 What did Del Boy use as a turban to wrap around one of the horse-riding hats?

....

1223 What was Rodney's new title in Trotters' Independent Traders in this episode: *Director of* .... ?

....

1224 Which one of Del Boy's mates did we also see in the hospital reception area at the end of the episode?

....

FEATURE-LENGTH SPECIALS – 2

1225 In 'Fatal Extraction', what country manufactured the video cameras that Del Boy was selling?

....

...

1226 In 'Rodney Come Home', what type of disease did Uncle Albert say he might get by eating hamburgers from the shopping centre?

....

1227 In 'To Hull and Back', what airline had just announced the arrival of a flight from Amsterdam at the beginning of the episode?

....

1228 In 'The Frog's Legacy', what British female TV presenter and singer's name did Del Boy use to describe his back?

....

1229 In 'Dates', what country did Uncle Albert say had invaded Singapore, thereby leading to the loss of the papers relating to his court marshall?

....

1230 In 'Miami Twice: The American Dream', which Eastern European city did Rodney tell Del Boy that Racquel had told him Del Boy received a telephone call from the previous evening?

....

1231 In 'Heroes and Villains', what 'England Football Song' were Del Boy and Rodney singing when Rodney told Del Boy that Cassandra was going to have a baby?

....

1232 In 'The Jolly Boys' Outing', what was the 'Science & Nature' question that Del Boy was asked during a game of Trivial Pursuit?

....

1233 In 'Modern Men', what famous British motorbike rider did Del Boy say the Indian community would be riding around on their bikes like if they wore his new-style crash helmet?

....

1234 In 'Miami Twice: Oh To Be In England', how did Del Boy almost get lost out at sea?

....

'TIME ON OUR HANDS' 1

1235   What type of book do we see Racquel reading at the beginning of the episode?

....

1236   When Racquel's parents rang the doorbell everyone, except Uncle Albert, started to panic. What '*convoys*' did Uncle Albert claim they would have been no use in during the War?

....

1237   How did Uncle Albert manage to mess up the gravy for the dinner?

....

1238   Can you recall the name of the TV presenter that Del Boy told Rodney to leave *This Is Your Life* to?

....

1239 What type of '*lubricating oil*' was Del Boy going to spray on the watch to clean it before Racquel's father stopped him from doing so?

....

1240 What did Del Boy name the house he purchased from his share of the money?

....

1241 What did Del Boy buy Uncle Albert from his share of the money?

....

1242 Where did Del Boy, Rodney and Uncle Albert all meet up for one last visit at the end of the episode?

....

1243 When Del Boy took a telephone call in the empty flat what '*household cleaning appliance*' was one of his contacts attempting to sell him 400 of?

....

1244 What '*markets*' did Del Boy try and convince Rodney to invest his share of the money in?

....

'TIME ON OUR HANDS' – 2

1245   What type of meat was Racquel cooking for the dinner she was preparing for her parents' visit?

....

1246   What skin affliction did Del Boy say the 15-year-old bottle of Port that Racquel's father bought for dinner might have?

....

1247   What was the Christian name of Racquel's Father – James, Jeremy or John?

....

1248   Prior to Del Boy and Rodney going to the auction rooms they were in The Nag's Head. What type of Eastern European car did Boycie say he would sell both of them on their way back from the auction?

....

1249 What was the name of the famous Indian leader that Trigger said made one good movie and then we never saw him again?

....

1250 What was the name of the auction rooms that the timepiece was sold in?

....

1251 To the nearest £1 million, how much was the timepiece (*watch*) actually sold for?

....

1252 What game could we see Del Boy playing in his home just before he decided to pay the flat one last visit?

....

1253 When Del Boy was dreaming in the empty flat, he heard his mum tell him to get up and go to school even if he had a hangover because he had an exam to take. What exam was mentioned?

....

1254 At the end of the episode, Del Boy told Rodney that this time next year they would be ....? What did he say?

....

'IF THEY COULD SEE US NOW' – 1

1255 What museum did Rodney say they had considered donating the valuable watch they had found to?

....

1256 When we saw a superimposed photograph of Del Boy and Rodney outside Peckham General Hospital, name either one of the two people the Boys were standing next to.

....

1257 Can you name the hotel or the Christian name of the hotel manager that we saw the Trotter Clan book into?

....

1258 Who had Uncle Albert gone to live with?

....

1259 What was the name of the Ricky Martin song we could hear playing in the background when we saw the Trotter Clan on Concorde?

....

1260 Who or what did Cassandra want Rodney to dress up as?

....

1261 What was the name of the quiz show that Del Boy appeared on?

....

1262 What was the '*title*' of the question that Del Boy was asked about a Robin Reliant: Banker, Decider or Penalty?

....

1263 Who suggested to Rodney that Del Boy should have used Trigger as his '*SOS*' in place of Rodney?

....

1264 What did Del Boy tell the producer of the quiz show to do with the money he had won?

....

'IF THEY COULD SEE US NOW' – 2

1265 Name any one of the four previous episodes of *Only Fools and Horses* we saw a clip from when Rodney was thinking back over the years?

....

1266 What embarrassing thing did Del Boy and Rodney (along with Cassandra, Damien and Racquel) do when they heard Uncle Albert had passed away?

....

1267 What court did Del Boy and Rodney have to appear in over the monies they owed?

....

1268 Name any two of the four character witnesses who turned up at court to testify on behalf of Del Boy and Rodney.

....

1269   When Mickey Pearce was winding Rodney up with a phone call,
       Mickey pretended he was representing the Sultan of ....
       Can you recall the country?

       ....

1270   What was the name of the Kylie Minogue song we could hear
       playing in the background when Del Boy and Rodney were sitting
       chatting in a bar?

       ....

1271   What did Rodney want Cassandra to dress up as?

       ....

1272   What was the minimum or maximum amount of money that a
       contestant could win on the quiz show?

       ....

1273   Who hosted the quiz show that Del Boy appeared on?

       ....

1274   What did Del Boy say Ravel made when he told Rodney that
       the question he had been asked on the quiz show was a trick
       question?

       ....

'STRANGERS ON THE SHORE – 1

1275 What was Del Boy doing at the very beginning of this spisode?

....

1276 What famous comic did Damien describe Rodney as being better than?

....

1277 What famous Reggae singer's name did Del Boy use when he mentioned the name of a nearby state?

....

1278 What type of '*gas fires*' was Del Boy keen Trotters Independent Traders should purchase a number of?

....

1279 What '*cooking flavouring*' did Del Boy use to replace Boycie's hair gel?

....

1280 What type of '*bag*' did Del Boy tell Rodney not to scatter Uncle Albert's ashes like?

....

1281 Can you recall what country's National Anthem Del Boy said was being played when he and Rodney arrived at the little French town?

....

1282 What did Denzil and Trigger think they had found in the back of the van when they were unloading the crates of beer?

....

1283 What Christian name did Del Boy give to the person in No. 1282?

....

1284 What terrorist organisation did Denzil say the young man who was in the back of his van could have been a member of?

....

'STRANGERS ON THE SHORE – 2

1285   What type of car did Marlene ask Del Boy to clean for her?

....

1286   Which one of Del Boy's business acquaintances was attempting
        to sell Del Boy some gas fires?

....

1287   What did Damien fire at Uncle Albert's urn?

....

1288   What '*male operation*' did Del Boy say could be reversed quicker
        than the time it took Rodney to reverse the van?

....

1289 Who was sitting beside Trigger at the bar in The Nag's Head?

....

1290 What was Del Boy wearing on his head when we saw him in the van in France?

....

1291 Who drove the forklift containing all the crates of beer and loaded it on to the back of Denzil's van?

....

1292 What did Del Boy say when he heard that Denzil and Trigger had found a young man in the back of Denzil's van? (Clue: Famous Paris street.)

....

1293 What belonging to Del Boy did Rodney give the young man to wear that led Damien to say that he looked like a set of traffic lights?

....

1294 At the end of the episode who called to the flat asking Del Boy to put him up for the night because his house was unsafe to stay in?

....

'SLEEPLESS IN PECKHAM' – 1

1295 What '*money sign*' made from gold was Damien wearing on a chain when we saw him at the beginning of the episode?

....

1296 Name either one of the three things Del Boy asked Damien whether he was sure he had when Damien was leaving the flat to go to school?

....

1297 Which one of Del Boy's mates did Damien suggest had '*ran off* with Marlene?

....

1298 What government agency was going to sell the flat to recoup monies Del Boy owed?

....

1299 What did Rodney say he was writing when we saw him sitting at the table with a laptop computer?

....

1300 Name either one of the two types of beer can we could see lying on Del Boy and Rodney's mum's grave.

....

1301 Who did Rodney discover was his real father in this episode?

....

1302 Why did a law firm continually write to Del Boy and Rodney in an effort to get them to visit the law firm?

....

1303 When Rodney saw his daughter for the first time he turned to Del Boy and said she '*was like a work of* ....' What did he say?

....

1304 What Christian name did Rodney give his baby girl?

....

'SLEEPLESS IN PECKHAM' – 2

1305 Name either of the two things that Cassandra had a 'food craving' for when she was pregnant.

....

1306 What did Del Boy say Cassandra needed more than a midwife when he said her baby would shoot out of her?

....

1307 What '*device*' was Trigger working on that he said he would patent for Del Boy?

....

1308 Name the male actor that Rodney said he would like to play the leading role in his movie.

....

1309 When Rodney told Del Boy about the success of the *Harry Potter* books, Del Boy suggested that Rodney should write a similar story called *Harry* ....?

....

1310 Why had Marlene not been seen for more than ten days?

....

1311 What song by Travis could we hear being played when Rodney left the camera shop and also when he was in the restaurant with Cassandra?

....

1312 Who offered Del Boy a place to stay if the flat was sold?

....

1313 What did Rodney say he was going to ask for if he was sent to prison?

....

1314 Complete the name of the solicitors who wrote out to Del Boy and Rodney: Cartwright, Cartwright & ....?

....

MIXED BAG – 15

1315 In 'The Yellow Peril', what make of luxurious car did Del Boy tell Rodney he would give him one of if Del had two?

....

1316 In 'Strained Relations', name either of the two mixers that Del Boy ordered in The Nag's Head with his Malibu.

....

1317 In 'Watching the Girls Go By', where did Del Boy and Rodney pretend they saw the stripper's snake hiding at the end of the episode?

....

1318 In 'As One Door Closes', who pulled up outside Nelson Mandela House looking for Del Boy and resulted in Del, Rodney and Uncle Albert fleeing the flat?

....

1319 In 'To Hull and Back', what did Del say he would be helping to reduce the cost of as a direct result of him smuggling diamonds into Britain?

....

1320 In 'The Longest Night', what department within the supermarket did Del Boy get the shoplifter a job in?

....

1321 In 'Tea For Three', why did Uncle Albert say he was reluctant to visit his wife in hospital?

....

1322 In 'Video Nasty', where did Del Boy say Mickey Pearce was filming a wedding when Uncle Albert asked Rodney Mickey's whereabouts?

....

1323 In 'Who Wants To Be A Millionaire?', what type of rug did Del Boy have at the flat that required cleaning: Egyptian, Iranian or Persian?

....

1324 In 'A Royal Flush', Vicky described the county where she was born and brought up as 'boring'. Can you recall the county?

....

EXPERT: DEL BOY

1325 What is Del Boy's middle name?

....

1326 In 'The Long Legs of the Law', how did Del describe the streets where he and Rodney worked when he learned that Rodney was about to date a policewoman?

....

1327 In 'A Losing Streak', what did Del Boy say guys like him did in World War II?

....

1328 In 'The Yellow Peril', Del Boy came up with one of his foreign sayings. Can you complete it? '*Tres Bien* ....'

....

1329 In 'A Touch of Glass', Del Boy asked Rodney what musical he was expecting the musical cats to play. What was it?

....

1330 In 'Friday The 14th', when the Mad Axe Killer heard a helicopter flying overhead, who did Del Boy say it was?

....

1331 In 'Strained Relations', what famous sailor's name did Del Boy call Uncle Albert?

....

1332 In 'Sleeping Dogs Lie', what did Del Boy call out to Dukie to persuade him to come out from the back of the van?

....

1333 In 'To Hull and Back', what famous Naval officer did Del Boy refer to when he told Rodney that Uncle Albert was England's greatest sailor since the officer in question lost the Armada?

....

1334 In 'A Royal Flush', Del Boy started to sing the song from an opera. Can you recall the name of the song or the opera it was from?

....

1335 In 'Ashes to Ashes', can you recall the name of Rodney's girlfriend?

....

1336 In 'A Losing Streak', how much, to the nearest 50 pence, did Rodney give Del to add to his stake money from the empty bottles he returned?

....

1337 In 'No Greater Love', what was the Christian name of the girl Rodney met at the roller disco?

....

1338 What is Rodney's middle name?

....

1339   In 'The Yellow Peril', Rodney claimed that the deep sea diver's
        watch Del Boy gave him was broken. What Asian city did Rodney
        say the watch told him it was '*chucking out time in*'?

....

1340   In 'May the Force Be with You', what was the Christian name of
        the girl Rodney was going out with?

....

1341   In 'Strained Relations', what pop group's album did Rodney
        suggest Del Boy play?

....

1342   In 'To Hull and Back', what glossy magazine was Rodney
        glancing through as he waited in the van for Del who was with
        Abdul and Boycie in the back of Denzil's lorry?

....

1343   In 'A Royal Flush', what College of Art did Rodney tell Vicky he
        went to?

....

1344   In 'Dates' Del Boy told Rodney that he was going out for lunch
        with an actress. What famous American actress did Rodney ask
        Del Boy if he was taking to lunch?

....

1345 In 'The Second Time Around', what was the name of Pauline Harris's husband?

....

1346 In 'A Slow Bus to Chingford', what was the name of the garage from where Del Boy got the loan of the open-top bus?

....

1347 What could Grandad be seen eating in the opening title pages to all of the episodes in Series 1?

....

1348 In 'The Russians are Coming', we learnt that Grandad had another brother in addition to Uncle Albert. What was his name?

....

1349   In 'Christmas Crackers' Grandad said that a Christmas card had
        arrived from 'Brenda, Terry, Shirley, Shane and ....'. Fill in
        the missing boy's name. (Clue: it begins with the letter 'S'.)

        ....

1350   In 'A Slow Bus to Chingford', a road sign could be seen lying on
        the floor in the flat. What did it say?

        ....

1351   In 'The Russians are Coming', what was the registration number
        of the police car (*the first three letters or the three numbers will
        be acceptable*)?

        ....

1352   Complete Rodney's line from 'The Second Time Around': '*Here
        today, gone this* ....'.

        ....

1353   In 'Christmas Crackers', what model of Rolls-Royce did Del Boy
        ask Rodney to pretend was owned by Del?

        ....

1354   In 'The Second Time Around', Pauline telephoned the speaking
        clock prior to vacating the flat. What country's speaking clock did
        she call and what boy's name did Grandad referred to the clock
as.   as.

        ....

EXPERT SERIES 2

1355 In 'The Long Legs of the Law', Rodney informed Grandad and Del Boy that he wouldn't be out too late because Sandra had to get up early the next morning. What did Rodney say Sandra was required to do?

....

1356 In 'Diamonds are for Heather', what song was being played when we watched Del and Darren go up and down in the children's boat ride?

....

1357 In 'Ashes to Ashes', what was the name of Trigger's granny?

....

1358 In 'A Losing Streak', what name was on the label of the bottles of dodgy perfume that Rodney and Grandad were making?

....

1359 In 'No Greater Love', name any of the two things Irene's husband was sent to jail for?

....

1360 In 'The Yellow Peril', name either of the two descriptions that Del Boy and Rodney gave the luminous paint when they were in the flat?

....

1361 In 'It Never Rains…', what was Rodney attempting to sell in the pouring rain in the market?

....

1362 In 'A Touch of Glass', what explanation did Lord Ridgemere offer as the reason why Van Gough chopped off one of his ears?

....

1363 In 'Diamonds are for Heather', what was the name of the flamenco singing duo at The Nag's Head?

....

1364 In 'No Greater Love', Rodney claimed that his latest girlfriend had such a good body that it would have made a famous Hollywood star consider plastic surgery. Name the actress Rodney mentioned.

....

EXPERT SERIES 3

1365 In 'Healthy Competition', what was the name of the Indian restaurant where Del went for a curry?

....

1366 In 'Wanted', name the two police departments that Del told Rodney had been outside The Nag's Head the previous evening?

....

1367 In 'May the Force Be with You', what did Del say Slater could be advertising in a few years time?

....

1368 In 'Friday The 14th', why did Del Boy think the police stopped them on their way to Boycie's cottage in Cornwall?

....

1369 In 'Yesterday Never Comes', Del suggested that Grandad go to his bedroom and watch TV. What TV programme did Del suggest Grandad watch?

....

1370 In 'May the Force Be with You', what type of poisoning did Grandad warn Slater that he would catch if he wasn't careful.

....

1371 In 'Wanted', what was the title of the Johnny Cash album that Del Boy played to wind up Rodney when he pretended the police were looking for him?

....

1372 In 'Friday The 14th', what street did Rodney own in the game of Monopoly?

....

1373 In 'Who's a Pretty Boy', what was the name of the Indian gentleman that Del spoke to in The Nag's Head?

....

1374 In 'Thicker than Water', Rodney joked that Del's girlfriend had spent two weeks in quarantine. From where did Rodney say she had entered Britain?

....

EXPERT SERIES 4

1375 In 'Happy Returns', what female pop singer's LP did Del Boy ask Junie if she wanted him to pop back to the flat and get?

....

1376 In 'As One Door Closes', what did Del Boy fall off in search of the rare butterfly?

....

1377 In 'Strained Relations', we were led to believe that Trigger nicked the cigarette machine from The Nag's Head. What brand were the vast majority of the packets of cigarettes that he gave Rodney in the flat?

....

1378 In 'Hole in One', Rodney suggested that they sell the van and get something more useful. What did Rodney suggest they purchase?

....

1379 In 'It's Only Rock 'n' Roll', Del Boy bought a load of damaged toy dolls. Can you recall any of the three things we heard the dolls say?

....

1380 In 'Happy Returns', what age was Rodney?

....

1381 In 'Sleeping Dogs Lie', what dog food television commercials did Del Boy say he had appeared on when he was talking to the lady in the park?

....

1382 In 'Watching the Girls Go By', from who did Rodney purchase his white jacket?

....

1383 In 'As One Door Closes', how many louvre doors was Del Boy purchasing?

....

1384 In 'Happy Returns', what was the name of Del's best mate's girlfriend?

....

1385 In 'From Prussia With Love', can you recall the name of the
famous jazz musician that Boycie said he could never convince
people was his Grandad when he saw the colour of Anna's baby?

....

1386 In 'The Miracle of Peckham', can you name the character, from a
children's story that Rodney referred to Uncle Albert as?

....

1387 In 'The Longest Night', can you recall the name of the casino
where Del Boy's date for the evening worked as a croupier?

....

1388 In 'Tea for Three', what name did Del Boy tell Trigger's niece that
he gave to her mum when they were younger?

....

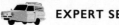

1389 In 'Video Nasty', what name did Del Boy initially give to his rhinoceros story?

....

1390 In 'Who Wants to Be a Millionaire?' what name did Del Boy give to the champagne that he ordered from Mike in The Nag's Head?

....

1391 In 'From Prussia with Love', apart from attempting to bribe a Lord Mayor, can you recall any one of the other four offences Boycie stated prevented him and Marlene from being able to adopt a baby.

....

1392 In 'The Longest Night', what luxury health appliance did the manager of the supermarket claim his wife had just obtained estimates for?

....

1393 In 'Tea For Three', what did Del Boy say to greet Rodney when Rodney returned to the table after getting the cheese from the kitchen in the flat?

....

1394 In 'Video Nasty', what was the name of the film that Rodney said Mickey Pearce wanted to make in the flat after Mickey's girlfriend started to take her clothes off?

....

1395 In 'Yuppy Love', Mickey Pearce asked Rodney if he had a pimple on top of something. What was it?

....

1396 In 'Danger UXD', what '*local name*' did Denzil plan to call his courier service until Del Boy persuaded him otherwise?

....

1397 In 'Chain Gang', what prevented Cassandra from telling Rodney that she loved him when she was in her car?

....

1398 In 'The Unlucky Winner Is…', what did Cassandra say she would take up when Rodney asked her if she would miss him when he went on holiday?

....

1399 In 'Sickness and Wealth', at the séance Elsie Partridge said that Del's mother was worried about his health. What did Del Boy claim was stuck somewhere in his stomach and that was the reason for him being in pain?

....

1400 In 'Little Problems', what did Boycie say two of Cassandra's bridesmaids were?

....

1401 In 'Yuppy Love', what was the name of the 'Avenue' where Rodney pretended to Cassandra that he lived?

....

1402 In 'Danger UXD', what English port did Del Boy just say he had got back from with 25 ten-kilo boxes of fresh Jersey tomatoes?

....

1403 In 'Chain Gang', what is Arnie drinking in the One Eleven Club when we first see him?

....

1404 In 'The Unlucky Winner Is…', why was Rodney not permitted to collect the money he won in the Spanish Lottery?

....

1405 In 'The Sky's The Limit', how did Racquel know that Del Boy was eating fried foods for breakfast again instead of grapefruit?

....

1406 In 'Chance Of A Lunchtime', what play by William Shakespeare did Del Boy tell Cassandra that Racquel was auditioning for?

....

1407 In 'Stage Fright', Del Boy told Uncle Albert that he ate on the move with a mobile phone in one hand. What did he say was in his other hand?

....

1408 In 'The Class of '62', when Del Boy said that some of his business acquaintances ran organisations that were household names, what prison did Rodney mention?

....

1409 In 'He Ain't Heavy, He's My Uncle', where did Racquel suggest
Rodney say he had been for ten years when they were talking
about how Rodney could explain how he had never paid any
taxes or National Insurance contributions?

....

1410 In 'Three Men, A Woman and A Baby', who did Rodney tell Del
Boy and Racquel had become a vegetarian?

....

1411 In 'The Sky's The Limit', where did Del Boy say Rodney looked
like he had just returned home from on a Club 18–30 trip?

....

1412 In 'Chance Of A Lunchtime', what part of Tyler's face did Del Boy
say Marlene's baby had that was similar to Trigger's?

....

1413 In 'Stage Fright', what was the Christian name of the manager
of the nightclub where Del Boy booked Racquel and Tony for a
cabaret act?

....

1414 In 'The Class of '62', what female writer did Del Boy liken to
'*Mr Kipling's bit on the side*'?

....

EXPERT: FEATURE-LENGTH SPECIALS – 1

1415 In 'The Jolly Boys' Outing', what caused the coach to explode?

....

1416 In 'Strangers on the Shore', can you recall what type of
hamburger Del Boy said Boycie's head would smell like after he
replaced his hair gel with onion purée?

....

1417 In 'Dates', Jevon could not understand why Mickey Pearce claimed
that Rodney was attractive to the opposite sex and described him
as not being a '*Master of the* ....' Can you fill in the
missingword?

....

1418 In 'The Frog's Legacy', when Del Boy discovered that the gold
bullion had been buried at sea, whose locker did he say he was
not going to allow it to stay in?

....

1419   In 'Sleepless in Peckham', name the female actress that Rodney
       said he would like to star in his movie.

       ....

1420   In 'To Hull and Back', what did Del Boy tell Rodney to '*look out for*'
       and '*listen out for*' when the boys were attempting to make their
       way to Holland?

       ....

1421   In 'Fatal Extraction', name the British male artist's LPs that Del Boy
       was selling in the market when he should have been at school
       taking his exams?

       ....

1422   In 'Modern Men', what type of job did Mickey Pearce tell Rodney
       he was starting: Double Glazing Salesman, Postman or Trainee
       Car Salesman?

       ....

1423   In 'Time on Our Hands', what popular make of coffee did Uncle
       Albert use as gravy granules by mistake?

       ....

1424   In 'Heroes and Villains', can you recall the name of the British
       cyclist that Del Boy said wore the cycling helmets he was
       attempting to sell in the market?

       ....

EXPERT: FEATURE-LENGTH SPECIALS – 2

1425 In 'Christmas Crackers', what did Del Boy say would revive the turkey Grandad had undercooked?

....

1426 In 'Diamonds are for Heather', what did Heather pour for her and Del to drink when they got back to her flat?

....

1427 In 'Thicker than Water', when Del Boy asked his father what a cubic foot was, what did Del Boy say his father said?

....

1428 In 'To Hull and Back', what did Slater say his nickname at the Metropolitan Police was?

....

1429 In 'A Royal Flush', who did Vicky say followed her everywhere she went?

....

1430 In 'The Frog's Legacy', what did Del Boy tell Mike that Trigger was still struggling with when Mike suggested that Trigger might be interested in purchasing a computer?

....

1431 In 'Dates', what did Del Boy describe Uncle Albert as being as cunning as?

....

1432 In 'The Jolly Boys' Outing', what '*Sea*' did Uncle Albert say he was sailing on when he was aboard a Greek herring trawler?

....

1433 In 'Rodney Come Home', what did Mickey tell a lady at the night club she reminded him of from his schooldays?

....

1434 In 'Miami Twice: The American Dream', who did Del Boy say the Vicar would have to '*square it off with*' when he was attempting to sell the church his pre-blessed communion wine?

....

EXPERT: FEATURE-LENGTH SPECIALS – 3

1435 In 'The Sky's The Limit', how much did Rodney pay for the hotel room and champagne?

....

1436 In 'To Hull and Back', what type of shadows did Rodney inform Del Boy he could do when Del asked him to think of a way of notifying him that the police were around?

....

1437 In 'Fatal Extraction', complete this Del Boy saying that he used when Rodney asked him if he could cheat on Racquel: '*Bonnet de ....*'

....

1438 In 'Chance of a Lunchtime', what make of sports car was in the painting which was hanging on the wall in the Trotters' flat?

....

1439 In 'Time on Our Hands', can you recall the name of the famous explorer Del Boy said he wanted to feel the same excitement as?

....

1440 In 'Heroes and Villains', who did Trigger think that Del Boy and Rodney looked like in their fancy dress costumes?

....

1441 In 'Stage Fright', which one of Del Boy's associates was selling reject three-piece suites?

....

1442 In 'Sleepless in Peckham', can you recall either one of the two tribute music acts (actual names or stage name used) that had been booked for Saturday nights at The Nag's Head?

....

1443 In 'He Ain't Heavy, He's My Uncle', how many carrier bags of groceries do we see sitting on the floor in the Trotters' flat at the beginning of the episode?

....

1444 In 'The Frog's Legacy' how did Freddie the Frog get his nickname?

....

EXPERT: 'A ROYAL FLUSH'

1445 What hotel was Del Boy looking for when he pretended to be a tourist in the market?

....

1446 What was the name of the opera that Del Boy got tickets for Rodney and Vicky to attend?

....

1447 What type of *finishing school* did Vicky tell Rodney she had gone to?

....

1448 What age was Vicky when her Mother died?

....

1449 Who did Rodney tell Del Boy he would not turn into by merely wearing a green pair of Wellington boots?

....

1450 When Del Boy, Rodney and Uncle Albert entered the gun shop, the shop assistant asked Del Boy what his pleasure was. What two things did Del Boy say he liked?

....

1451 What was the name of the Duke's horse that was entered in The Derby?

....

1452 Who did Del Boy borrow the pump-action shotgun from to go clay pigeon shooting?

....

1453 What was the name of Vicky's family home in Berkshire?

....

1454 What was the only opera Rodney claimed that Del Boy had seen?

....

EXPERT: 'CHAIN GANG'

1455 Can you recall the name of the bouncer at the One Eleven Club?

....

1456 What was the surname of the businessman who proudly announced as he entered the One Eleven Club that he had gone into voluntary liquidation again?

....

1457 Where did Cassandra tell Rodney she was going for a course organised by her work?

....

1458 How much was each gold chain actually worth?

....

1459 Who did Arnie say he had obtained the chains for, only for this person to let him down?

....

1460 What was the first name of Arnie's wife?

....

1461 What part of London was the Italian restaurant located?

....

1462 Can you recall the name of the head waiter in the Italian restaurant?

....

1463 What was the name of the hospital where Rodney followed the ambulance before eventually losing it?

....

1464 Name either of Arnie's two sons?

....

EXPERT: 'DATES'

1465 At the beginning of the episode we saw a number of boxes piled up in the flat. Where did it say that the boxes had been made?

....

1466 What was the name of the submarine hunter that Uncle Albert served on and ended up sinking after he crashed it into a United States aircraft carrier?

....

1467 What was the name of the United States aircraft carrier?

....

1468 When Trigger walked into The Nag's Head wearing a blue suit and carrying a bunch of flowers for his blind date, what '*Day*' did Del Boy think it was?

....

1469 What was the name of the dating agency that both Trigger and Del Boy used?

....

1470 Where did Del Boy take Racquel for lunch on their blind date?

....

1471 What make of a Ford car did Boycie claim the Trotter Clan were in when they first arrived in Peckham?

....

1472 Can you recall the role Racquel said she had in the *Dr Who* episode she appeared in?

....

1473 What was the name of the pop group that Racquel and her friend formed when she was 17?

....

1474 When Del Boy was talking to Marlene on the telephone about a present for Uncle Albert's birthday, what did he suggest she buy him?

....

EXPERT: 'DANGER UXD'

1475 What make of video recorder was written on the box at the start of the episode?

....

1476 What was the name of the business programme that Del Boy asked Rodney to record for him when he was out?

....

1477 Mike served Denzil a bowl of stew and charged him £1. What did he charge the '*yuppy*' for his Beef Bourguignon?

....

1478 Can you name either of the two yuppies who were in The Nag's Head when Del Boy walked in?

....

1479   What was the name of Del Boy and Rodney's neighbour who passed them outside Nelson Mandela House?

....

1480   How much did Del Boy offer to sell the dolls to '*Dirty Barry*' for?

....

1481   What was the name of the company that Denzil collected the dolls from?

....

1482   Can you recall the name of the German city that Boycie mentioned when he was asked if the video recorders had fallen off the back of a lorry?

....

1483   What reason did Rodney think was responsible for the two dolls self-inflating?

....

1484   Can you recall the name given to either of the two dolls?

....

EXPERT:
MIXED BAG – 1

1485 In 'The Yellow Peril', Del Boy said goodbye to Mr Chin with
'*Sianora*' and what other words that sound similar to a Chinese
restaurant dish?

....

1486 In 'No Greater Love', how much was Rodney allowing Irene to
pay back per week of the £17 she owed him for clothes?

....

1487 In 'It Never Rains…', what was the name of the girl that Del Boy
met at the bar beside the pool in Benidorm?

....

1488 In 'Diamonds Are for Heather', what was the first name of Heather's babysitter?

....

1489 In 'May the Force Be with You', what was the nickname of the boy who sat on Trigger's face at school while Del Boy and his mates poured itching powder over him?

....

1490 In 'Wanted', what '*bad day*' description did Del Boy give to the breakfast Grandad cooked for him?

....

1491 In 'Who's a Pretty Boy', how much did Grandad pay the pet shop owner for the canary?

....

1492 In 'Thicker than Water', what job did Reggie have at Newcastle Infirmary?

....

1493 What was Uncle Albert's full character name?

....

1494 In 'It's Only Rock 'n' Roll', at what number did Rodney's former group enter the pop charts when they appeared on *Top of the Pops*?

....

EXPERT: MIXED BAG – 2

1495 In 'Watching the Girls Go By', what was the Christian name of the stripper Del Boy fixed Rodney up with?

....

1496 In 'From Prussia With Love', what type of boots did Boycie say would be heard around his home after he learned that the mother of the baby was born in Germany?

....

1497 In 'The Longest Night', what was the Christian name of the shoplifter's Mother?

....

1498 In 'Tea For Three', why did Trigger's niece pay him a visit?

....

1499 In 'Video Nasty', what was the name of the person Del Boy spoke to on the telephone at the Chinese takeaway?

....

1500 In 'Hole in One', what colour jumper was Del Boy wearing when their solicitor was briefing them about Uncle Albert's claim against the brewery?

....

1501 In 'Thicker than Water', Grandad and Rodney were wearing paper hats. Can you recall the colour of either of the hats?

....

1502 In 'Strained Relations', Uncle Albert said he had lived with Patsy's girl for a while. Can you recall Patsy's daughter's Christian name?

....

1503 In 'It Never Rains…', where in Peckham did Grandad say the Trotter Family lived in 1936?

....

1504 In 'Diamonds are for Heather', what was the name of the Indian restaurant where Del Boy put the engagement ring on the table?

....

ANSWERS

CHRISTMAS SPECIALS

1.	'The Jolly Boys Outing'	1989
2.	'Diamonds are for Heather'	1982
3.	'A Royal Flush'	1986
4.	'Mother Nature's Son'	1992
5.	'Christmas Crackers'	1981
6.	'Dates'	1988
7.	'Heroes and Villains'	1996
8.	'To Hull and Back'	1985
9.	'The American Dream'	1991 (Miami Twice: PI)
10.	'The Frog's Legacy'	1987
11.	'Rodney Come Home'	1990
12.	'Thicker than Water'	1983
13.	'Oh To Be In England'	1991 (Miami Twice: PII)
14.	'Fatal Extraction'	1993

 **ANSWERS**

FIND THE EPISODE

15. 'Tea For Three'
16. 'Wanted'
17. 'The Second Time Around'
18. 'May the Force Be With You'
19. 'Diamonds are for Heather'
20. 'The Long Legs of the Law'
21. 'A Touch of Glass'
22. 'The Yellow Peril'
23. 'In Sickness and Wealth
24. 'Stage Fright'

MATCH THE EPISODE WITH THE SERIES

25.	'Danger UXD'	Series 6
26.	'Ashes to Ashes'	Series 2
27.	'Cash and Curry'	Series 1
28.	'The Class of '62'	Series 7
29.	'Hole in One'	Series 4
30.	'Friday The 14th'	Series 3
31.	'The Miracle of Peckham'	Series 5

DEL BOY – 1

32. David White – he later changed it to David Jason
33. Clive Dunn – Lance Corporal Jack Jones
34. London
35. 'Open All Hours'
36. Granville
37. 'Do Not Adjust Your Set'
38. A Trainee Mechanic
39. True – he played a gardener in the series in 1969
40. Blanco Webb
41. False – it was in *The Top Secret Life of Edgar Briggs*

RODNEY

42. Nicholas Lyndhurst
43. *Butterflies*
44. Adam
45. True, he played both parts
46. Two
47. Maths and Art
48. 'The Long Legs of the Law'
49. False, however he did play Ronnie Barker's son, Raymond, in the follow-up to *Porridge, Going Straight*
50. Charlton (*after the Football Team, Charlton Athletic*)
51. Chairman (*Vice-Chairman to Chairman in one go*)

I KNOW WHAT IT'S CALLED – 1

52. 'Thicker than Water'
53. 'The Second Time Around'
54. 'Stage Fright'
55. 'A Losing Streak'
56. 'Chain Gang'
57. 'Class Of '62'
58. 'Big Brother'
59. 'Hole in One'
60. 'The Yellow Peril'

WHO PLAYED WHO?

61. *Marlene* — Sue Holderness
62. *Sid (Sid's Café)* — Roy Heather
63. *Grandad* — Lennard Pearce
64. *Denzil* — Paul Barber
65. *Mike* — Kenneth MacDonald
66. *Damien* — Jamie Smith
67. *Uncle Albert* — Buster Merryfield

 **ANSWERS**

68.	*Trigger*	Roger Lloyd Pack
69.	*Mickey*	Patrick Murray
70.	*Racquel*	Tessa Peake-Jones
71.	*Jevon*	Steven Woodcock
72.	*Alan Parry*	Denis Lill
73.	*Boycie*	John Challis
74.	*Cassandra*	Gwyneth Strong

MIXED BAG – 1
75. John Sullivan
76. *The Only Fools and Horses Story*
77. Sir Anthony Hopkins
78. 'Big Brother'
79. 1981
80. An axe
81. Joyce
82. Trigger's
83. An urn
84. True

MUSIC FROM THE SERIES
85. 'Who's a Pretty Boy?'
86. 'From Prussia With Love'
87. 'Yuppy Love'
88. 'Go West Young Man'
89. 'Miami Twice' ('Part Two – Oh To Be In England')
90. 'Stage Fright'
91. 'The Jolly Boys' Outing'
92. 'The Unlucky Winner Is…'
93. 'Video Nasty'
94. 'Cash and Curry'

SERIES 1 – PART 1

95. Seven
96. 'Christmas Crackers'
97. Trigger
98. E-type Jaguar
99. Three tonnes of lead
100. 'Chingford'
101. One
102. Pauline Harris
103. Beachwear for him and his Mrs
104. Trotters Ethnic Tours

MICKEY PEARCE

105. *The Bill*
106. *Little Problems*
107. Mobile telephones
108. False, it was a Pizza Hut advertisement
109. Three
110. 'Healthy Competition'
111. Lawnmower engines (broken!)
112. His hat
113. 50 pence
114. *Scum*

'BIG BROTHER'

115. Rodney (lying on the couch reading)
116. 25 vinyl briefcases
117. £200 (£8 per case)
118. Grandad had asked Rodney to get him an Emperor Burger from the Take-Away but Rodney couldn't afford one and brought him home a Cheeseburger. Grandad hated Cheeseburgers.

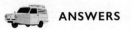 **ANSWERS**

119. Dan Dare
120. Millwall
121. Hong Kong
122. St Tropez
123. A doss house in Stoke Newington
124. He left his passport in the flat

MIXED BAG – 2

125. 'Go West Young Man'
126. Ray Butt
127. Nelson Mandela House
128. Reliant Regal Supervan III
129. New York – Paris – Peckham
130. True
131. *'S'il vous plait'* – in Series 1, Episode 1, 'Big Brother'
132. 13
133. Ford Cortina GT Convertible – in Series 1,
     Episode 2, 'Go West Young Man'
134. Six

HOOKY GEAR

135. Women's clothing   'No Greater Love'
136. Louvre doors   'As One Door Closes'
137. Secondhand cars   'Go West Young Man'
138. Lawn Mower Engines 'Healthy Competition'
139. Paint   'The Yellow Peril'
140. Lead   'The Miracle of Peckham'
141. A Baby   'From Prussia With Love'
142. Briefcases   'Big Brother'
143. Ethnic tours   'A Slow Bus to Chingford'
144. Blow-up dolls   'Danger UXD'

MIXED BAG – 3

145. Spain
146. A group of weekend fishermen
147. 'Heather'
148. Gas – he said Grandad was an out-of-work lamplighter
149. Tyler
150. 'A Touch Of Frost'
151. True
152. 'Crocodile Shoes'
153. Aubrey
154. A bus conductor (*to add a bit of glamour*)

SLATER

155. 'May The Force Be With You'
156. Roy
157. Rodney invited him home
158. A microwave oven
159. False, he used to be Racquel's husband
160. 'To Hull and Back'
161. Diamonds
162. Terry Hoskins
163. 'The Class Of '62'
164. He worked for an undertaker

'GO WEST YOUNG MAN'

165. Monica
166. Mickey Pearce – two weeks
167. Ford (*Cortina GT Convertible*)
168. £199
169. Sebastian Coe
170. 23,000
171. A Bible (*he claimed a Vicar was the previous owner*)

172. A Caribbean stallion
173. He recalled Reg Varney ordering half a lager in
      Holiday On The Buses
174. A cigar packet that Rodney threw out of the car on
      their way home

DEL BOY'S FOREIGN LINGO

175. *Nouvel*
176. *Au Revoir*
177. *Technik*
178. *Fabrique*
179. *Idiot*
180. *Tante*
181. *Alfredo Di Stefano* (he also used '*Puskas*' but
      he was born in Hungary)
182. *Bonjour*
183. *Plonker*
184. *Pucker*

DENZIL

185. Liverpool
186. *The Boys From The Blackstuff*
187. Long distance lorry driver
188. 'Who's a Pretty Boy?'
189. Corrine
190. A jam sponge
191. *Danger UXD*
192. *The Full Monty*
193. Horse
194. False

'CASH AND CURRY'

195. Vauxhall Velox

196. Vimol Malik and Mr Ram

197. A red belt in origami

198. A spoon

199. Kuera

200. Hindu God Of Wealth

201. India's premier wicket keeper

202. A Victorian globe

203. 'Bacon and Egg'

204. 27

No. 1 HITS – 1

205. 'Do You Really Want To Hurt Me' – 'Ashes to Ashes'
(28 October, 1982)

206. '2 Become 1' – 'Time On Our Hands'
(29 December, 1996)

207. 'Caravan Of Lov'e – 'A Royal Flush' (25 December, 1986)

208. 'Tainted Love' – 'Big Brother'
(8 September, 1981)

209. 'Especially For You' – 'Danger UXD' (15 January, 1989)

210. 'Uptown Girl' – 'Friday The 14th'
(24 November, 1983)

211. 'Only You' – 'Who's a Pretty Boy?'
(22 December, 1983)

212. 'Something's Gotten Hold Of My Heart' – 'Sickness and Wealth
(5 February, 1989)

213. 'Prince Charming' – 'A Slow Bus to Chingford' (6 October, 1981)

214. 'Saving All My Love For You' – 'To Hull and Back'
(25 December, 1985)

 **ANSWERS**

MIXED BAG – 4

215. £200
216. A Ferrari
217. £2,000
218. Series 4 (Episode 2 – 'Strained Relations')
219. Dave
220. Millionaires
221. Ajax (*Ajax Amsterdam*)
222. Lledo
223. 25
224. A chunky identity bracelet

UNCLE ALBERT – 1

225. Buster Merryfield
226. 'Strained Relations'
227. The toilet
228. A duffle coat
229. 'War'
230. He was a bank manager (*Nat West Bank, Thames Ditton Branch*)
231. True
232. Rum (*although Buster was teetotal in real life*)
233. False, Grandad was older than Albert
234. 'During The War............And Other Encounters'

GRANDAD

235. Lennard Pearce
236. Three
237. His false teeth
238. 'A Slow Bus to Chingford'
239. True
240. The Community Centre
241. The Christmas Pudding

242. Three
243. 'It Never Rains…' and 'May The Force Be With You'
244. Trigger's Grandmother

'THE SECOND TIME AROUND'

245. Trigger
246. Diesel oil
247. '*cemetery*'
248. Air-hostess
249. The Hollies
250. Because Ryan O'Neal didn't die
251. '*gold*'
252. *Pas De Calais*
253. Trigger
254. Auntie Rose's house in Clacton

'A SLOW BUS TO CHINGFORD'

255. Janice
256. Her bra
257. 'Chelsea'
258. Del couldn't understand why someone would want to make a statue of a disabled person
259. £5
260. 'Dracula'
261. Trotter Watch
262. A traffic warden's
263. She had a Corgi named 'Nero'
264. £17 (*included lunch*)

'THE RUSSIANS ARE COMING'

265. A Nuclear Fallout Shelter
266. 4

267. Peckham New Forest
268. A Ford Escort
269. Eric and Wayne
270. Corfu
271. On top of Nelson Mandela House
272. Grandad
273. Paving stones
274. 12

'CHRISTMAS CRACKERS'

275. Grandad
276. Glow Worms
277. The jiblets
278. A circus
279. Silver
280. The Monte Carlo Club
281. *The Sound Of Music*
282. Cream soda
283. A pen (*Relay*)
284. White

SERIES 1 – PART 2

285. *'Exchange and Mart'*
286. Sweden
287. Weed killer
288. Michelangelo
289. False (*the bloke who Del sold the Ford Cortina to smashed into him*)
290. A muzzle
291. Jamaican
292. Steak
293. 'Wallies'
294. 'A big scruff'

'THE LONG LEGS OF THE LAW'

295. In his mouth
296. Watches
297. Bacon
298. A Steradent tablet (for his false teeth)
299. Rodney said that Chelsea had dropped three points on Saturday
300. Greavsie (*Jimmy Greaves*)
301. Sandra
302. 'The Exterminator'
303. A packet of biscuits and a cup of tea
304. 'Bacteria'

NO. 1 HITS – 2

305. 'Don't You Want Me' – 'Christmas Crackers'
     (28 December, 1981)
306. 'Mr Blobby' – 'Fatal Extraction'
     (29 December, 1993)
307. 'You Spin Me Round' – 'Sleeping Dogs Lie'
     (21 March 1985)
308. 'Knockin' On Heaven's Door' – 'Heroes and Villains'
     (25 December, 1996)
309. 'I Know Him So Well' – 'Strained Relations'
     (28 February, 1985)
310. 'Innuendo' – 'He Ain't Heavy He's My Uncle'
     (27 January, 1991)
'311. I Don't Wanna Dance' – 'The Yellow Peril'
     (18 November, 1982)
312. 'Pass The Dutchie' – 'The Long Legs of the Law'
     (21 October, 1982)
313. '3am Eternal' – 'Three Men, A Woman and A Baby''
     (3 February, 1991)
314. 'Do They Know It's Christmas?' – 'The Jolly Boys' Outing'
     (25 December, 1989)

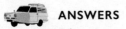 **ANSWERS**

DEL BOY – 2

315. Pink furry slippers
316. 'twonk'
317. Charles Aznavour
318. A mod
319. Nocturnal Security Officer
320. Joanie
321. Horse racing (*on at 2.30pm*)
322. 'inch'
323. (i) A well dressed man (ii) A steak meal (iii) Care and Consideration
324. Harris

'ASHES TO ASHES'

325. 'Tights'
326. 50 pence
327. As a copy
328. Ireland
329. Del Boy exclaimed *'Isn't that the black bloke that won Wimbledon'?*
330. Trigger's grandfather
331. True
332. The river police
333. Buddhists
334. A council dust lorry swept them up from the side of the road (*Del set them down while he and Rodney were having a rest and a chat*)

MIXED BAG – 5

335. 'Monitor'
336. Luton and Middlesbrough
337. '24 Hours From Tulsa' changed by Rodney to '24 Hours From Dartmoor'

338. Manuel (*Rodney*) & Juan (*Del*)
339. She decided to go back to her husband
340. Vespa (*Del used to be a Mod*)
341. Their dad
342. A Rolls-Royce
343. Denzil, Mickey Pearce and Rodney
344. Four

'IT NEVER RAINS…'
345. Pac-a-Mac
346. A Father's Day card
347. 80 per cent
348. Alex
349. Benidorm
350. A Traffic Violation – he was caught jaywalking
351. He was gun-running in Spain in 1936
352. Spanish Civil War
353. Grandad thought he was out looking for a car – Ford Consul
354. The 1982 World Cup Finals

CASSANDRA
355. Gwyneth Strong
356. False, she was born in East Ham, London
357. *A Touch Of Frost*
358. 'Yuppy Love'
359. 'The Unlucky Winner Is…'
360. Her bikini line
361. 'Modern Men'
362. She worked in a bank (*clerk*)
363. False
364. Parry

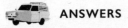 **ANSWERS**

'A TOUCH OF GLASS'

365. Three (*Del, Grandad and Rodney*)
366. Revolving Musical Cats
367. '*How Much Is That Doggy In The Window?*'
368. Battersea Dogs Home
369. Lady Ridgemere
370. Wallace
371. A cucumber sandwich and a cup of Earl Grey tea
372. 'Queer'
373. Cambridge
374. Cream Soda

SERIES 2 – PART 1

375. £1.25
376. Grandad's money
377. Because he had a GCE in Art
378. Cutlery he was attempting to steal
379. As *The Black November*
380. Vincent van Gogh (*Del pronounced his name as 'van Cough'*)
381. In his suitcase under his bed
382. 'Who pushed them and who picked them up'
383. Vadis
384. The roller disco

'DIAMONDS ARE FOR HEATHER'

385. £5
386. Laundrettes
387. Persil
388. Brixton
389. '*Rorke's Drift*'
390. Darren
391. Woks

392. *Billy Goat*
393. Captain
394. A Battleship

MIKE

395. Kenneth MacDonald
396. True
397. Fisher
398. *It Ain't Half Hot Mum*
399. Manchester
400. '*Who's a Pretty Boy?*'
401. Paint The Nag's Head
402. 1983 (Series 3, Episode 7 – 22 December 1983)
403. A Ford Escort XR3i
404. Certificates for his beer

'HOMESICK'

405. 'The London Marathon'
406. A waitress from the Pizza Palace
407. Trigger
408. 'No Smoking'
409. Vice-Chairman and then Chairman
410. 'Meeting Closed'
411. Euro Minister
412. Nijinsky
413. Oranges
414. Three

'HEALTHY COMPETITION'

415. Toy Puppy Dogs
416. £6
417. He said he was going on holiday

 **ANSWERS**

418. Gendarme
419. A pack of dogs
420. 24
421. Mickey Pearce
422. Broken lawnmower engines
423. Cut glass goblets
424. Egg and chips

NO. 1 HITS – 3

425. 'Save Your Love' – 'Diamonds are for Heather'
     (30 December, 1982)
426. 'Sadness Part 1' – 'The Class of '62'
     (20 January, 1991)
427. 'Don't Leave Me This Way' – 'The Longest Night'
     (14 September, 1986)
428. 'Saviour's Day' – 'The Sky's The Limit'
     (30 December, 1990)
429. 'Easy Lover' – 'Watching the Girls Go By'
     (28 March, 1985)
430. 'Always On My Mind' – 'The Frog's Legacy'
     (25 December, 1987)
431. 'I Will Always Love You' – 'Mother Nature's Son'
     (25 December, 1992)
432. 'Ice Ice Baby' – 'Rodney Come Home'
     (25 December, 1990)
433. 'I Want To Wake Up With You' – 'The Miracle of Peckham'
     (7 September, 1986)
434. 'Bohemian Rhapsody' – 'Miami Twice'
     (24 December, 1991)

MIXED BAG – 6

435. '*Happy Returns*'
436. £25
437. True
438. Rodney thought he carried a gun
439. Del Boy told Rodney he was called Trigger because he looked like a horse
440. 'A Tale Of Four Ports'
441. Nelson Mandela House
442. Harlech Tower (Park Road, East Acton, London)
443. 'The Longest Night'
444. False – we first see him in 'Thicker than Water'

RODNEY – 2

445. Moles
446. 13
447. Haddock
448. Plimsoles
449. Man at C & A
450. 'Cruffs'
451. A poof
452. Pork
453. *Gulliver's Travels*
454. Three

'FRIDAY THE 14th'

455. Fishing gear
456. Skiing
457. Boycie's
458. Cornwall (*Tregower*)
459. The police
460. As a typhoid (*Rodney said typhoon and Del thought he meant Typhoo tea*)

 **ANSWERS**

461. Scotch
462. Monopoly
463. The Mad Axe Killer
464. The Chief of Security at the nearby Institute

'YESTERDAY NEVER COMES'
465. Queen Anne
466. Woodworm
467. Rentokil
468. Miranda
469. As a 'Posh Tart'
470. Chelsea
471. Banana
472. On her bottom
473. The girl slapped him on the face
474. Del's grandmother (*although he claimed she left it to him*)

SERIES 2 – PART 2
475. Her wedding photograph
476. Black & White
477. Rodney had them on back to front as a result of his girlfriend's mum and dad arriving home unexpected
478. An old folks' home in Spain
479. CID
480. Dresden
481. Get his scissors out and trim it
482. He thought that there might be a spider in it
483. Ponce
484. A letter bomb

'MAY THE FORCE BE WITH YOU'

485. Trigger
486. Pink
487. Detective Inspector
488. A microwave oven
489. '*Treasure Island*' & '*Mutiny On The Bounty*'
490. A television
491. The au pair
492. True
493. A Jolly Roger flying from his chimney
494. A 'Moroccan Woodbine'

MIXED BAG 7

495. Granada
496. The Indian Restaurant
497. Shepherd's pie
498. A country lane – her car had broken down
499. 'Dix'
500. Courier/Tour Guide
501. Rodney said he had never smoked Astro Turf!
502. The John Player Special Team
503. Skateboard
504. Hamlet

'WANTED'

505. 'The Gruesome Twosome'
506. A bus
507. 'My Lovely'
508. 'Rape'
509. A doctor
510. Grandad (*he telephoned him at* The Nag's Head)
511. Under his bed

512. In the Tank Room at the top of Nelson Mandela House
513. A selection of tinned food
514. The Kebab House

'WHO'S A PRETTY BOY?'

515. 'Meter Out Of Order'
516. Brendan
517. Grey (*Battleship Grey*)
518. Denzil
519. A canary
520. Yellow
521. An apple
522. He wanted his living room re-decorated
523. 'Albino'
524. It died

'THICKER THAN WATER'

525. Rodney
526. Del Boy's latest girlfriend
527. 18
528. Newcastle
529. A hereditary blood disorder
530. Grapefruit
531. A large brandy each
532. Del Boy's
533. The zoo
534. A pizza

MIXED BAG – 8

535. A Renaissance Man
536. He pushed it
537. Salt & Vinegar

538. Elgin (*Elgin's Marbles*)
539. High and Low
540. Food poisoning
541. A portable toilet
542. One
543. 'Crossroads'
544. Sweden

'A LOSING STREAK'

545. Ethiopia
546. 'Tabby'
547. Boycie
548. £150
549. Rabbit's Foot
550. A double-headed coin
551. Boycie and Trigger
552. His 16th
553. Paul Daniels *(Heineken Beer Advertisements)*
554. The keys to his car

'NO GREATER LOVE'

555. Ladies clothing and camel hair coats
556. Singh
557. Bangladesh
558. Irene
559. Prison
560. 40
561. His knees
562. *Starsky & Hutch*
563. David, Daniel and Douglas
564. Morons

 **ANSWERS**

'THE YELLOW PERIL'

565. *'The Golden Lotus'*
566. Mr Chin
567. Paint the kitchen
568. Barclaycard
569. Planning permission
570. A black cat
571. *Sianora*
572. Deep sea diver's watch
573. £150
574. £75 – Del Boy, £40 – Rodney & £35 – Grandad

'HAPPY RETURNS'

575. An Adult Art Magazine
576. Rodney was dating the shop assistant behind the counter
577. The Green Cross Code
578. 50 pence
579. He let down the tyres on Del Boys three-wheel van
580. Junie
581. He was dating the daughter of Del's former fiancée (*No. 580*)
582. Duran Duran – 'Rio'
583. 19
584. Hai Kai Do

'STRAINED RELATIONS'

585. A hat
586. The Vicar who conducted Grandad's funeral ceremony
587. Trigger
588. Car batteries
589. North London
590. Uncle Albert
591. Because it tasted nice and wasn't burnt

(Grandad usually burnt everything he cooked)

592. Zebedee (from *The Magic Roundabout*)
593. Open The Nag's Head early
594. A hospital (London's Ear, Nose & Throat Hospital)

'HOLE IN ONE'

595. The cellar at The Nag's Head
596. Sun tan lotion
597. £500
598. A Jinx
599. Cross-cancelling
600. Four-dozen bottles of Guinness
601. Solly Atwell
602. The Jimmy Saville of Peckham
603. The Black Hole of Calcutta
604. He wanted to get some money to purchase Grandad's headstone

'IT'S ONLY ROCK 'N' ROLL'

605. Drummer
606. 'Ringo'
607. 'A Bunch Of Wallies'
608. Talking Dolls
609. Taiwan
610. The Shamrock Club
611. Duran Duran (pronounced 'Durum Durum' by Del Boy)
612. *Top of the Pops*
613. 'Boys Will Be Boys'
614. Mental Mickey

MIXED BAG – 9

615. Jet Lag
616. Sausages and Mash

617.   Mickey Pearce
618.   'Man'
619.   A Forged Bus Pass
620.   Pinocchio
621.   Bostik
622.   'A Tube of Signal' *(toothpaste)* & 'A Jam Sandwich'
623.   Nijinsky
624.   Mr Kipling

'SLEEPING DOGS LIE'
625.   A horror film
626.   The Seychelles
627.   £60
628.   Dukie
629.   A Great Dane
630.   His vitamin pill
631.   A new carpet (the lady's dog kept tearing holes in her carpet)
632.   Pork
633.   He had eaten the same pork that Del and Rodney fed the dog
634.   Scatty Mare

'WATCHING THE GIRLS GO BY'
635.   Boycie
636.   The Pizza Palace
637.   £2.50
638.   50 pence
639.   Rabbit (Del said that Mickey had too much 'rabbit')
640.   White Jacket, black shirt and white Tie
641.   A Liquorice Allsort
642.   In his Wranglers
643.   Helga
644.   Del paid a stripper to go with him

'AS ONE DOOR CLOSES'

645. Louvre Doors
646. £2,000
647. Rare butterflies
648. Deluxe trimming combs
649. £1.50
650. Denzil
651. It was is redundancy money
652. Lester Piggott
653. The Co-Op
654. *Love Story*

'TO HULL AND BACK'

655. Amsterdam
656. Lucozade
657. Digital watches
658. Japan
659. £15
660. Abdul
661. Take a briefcase of money to Amsterdam and smuggle diamonds back into Britain
662. Trigger
663. £10,000
664. Chief Inspector

'FROM PRUSSIA WITH LOVE'

665. Swedish
666. French
667. German
668. Anna
669. Rodney
670. Language

671. '*Au Revoir*'
672. A cabbage
673. He was going to sell the baby to Boycie and Marlene
674. Boris Becker

'THE MIRACLE OF PECKHAM'

675. A Trumpet
676. Lynda Evans who played Crystal Carrington
677. Dredges
678. He threw it down the dust shoot
679. Del Boy's after shave (Brut)
680. Church
681. He bought the lead that was stolen from its roof
682. The Hospice
683. £250,000
684. Uri Geller

'THE LONGEST NIGHT'

685. £1,000
686. The Head of Security for the supermarket stopped them on a false shoplifting charge
687. To the manager's office
688. A packet of frozen peas
689. 'The Shadow'
690. 6.00pm
691. £60,000
692. A heart attack
693. The Manager and the Head of Security
694. The toy department at the supermarket

'TEA FOR THREE'

695. Trigger
696. His wife (*Aida*)
697. Trigger's
698. A singing contest
699. Uncle Albert
700. £1
701. A home solarium
702. Cheese
703. Hang-Glide
704. The Paratroopers

MIXED BAG – 10

705. The Moonies
706. She asked him if he had been ill
707. His dirty books
708. Scurvy
709. Trigger said his Granny's wheelchair had a squeaky wheel
710. He got a lady to sew up the holes and he flogged them to some West Indian lads at the youth centre as soppy hats
711. A storm brought down all the power lines in the area including the institute's security system
712. Bull, cow and sheep
713. 'Wot (*pronounced 'Vot'*) Is Your Name?'
714. Foreign

'VIDEO NASTY'

715. Boycie and Trigger
716. Boycie
717. The Arts Council
718. Mickey Pearce
719. A seagull

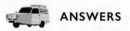**ANSWERS**

720. A typewriter
721. A rhinoceros
722. Weddings and Christenings
723. £50
724. 'A Jaffa'

DEL BOY – 3

725. Brighton
726. His last Polo Mint
727. The Ten Commandments
728. The medical [rofession
729. £95
730. Kermit (*the Frog*)
731. Cinderella
732. The Tally Man
733. Boots
734. Norway

RODNEY – 3

735. The Council
736. Washing her hair and mending her bike
737. Lourdes
738. A fascist
739. A prescription
740. Gigolos
741. Grapes
742. A Doberman Pinscher
743. His hair (*Del cut a chunk of his hair off at the market to demonstrate how sharp the trimming combs he was selling were*)
744. A prophet

UNCLE ALBERT – 2

745.   18 months
746.   In Uncle Albert's mouth
747.   Dukie's vitamin tablets
748.   Nein (*the German word for 'No'*)
749.   A kipper
750.   The Casting Couch
751.   The Entertainments Officer on 'The General Belgrano'
752.   £2,000
753.   A stick
754.   Cliff Richard

DEL BOY'S PALS

755.   Five-Card Draw
756.   A storage shed at a railway station
757.   Trigger
758.   They both thought she was a pretty girl
759.   Los Angeles
760.   Rollerboots
761.   Boycie
762.   Mike and Trigger
763.   20
764.   Carlsberg

SERIES 3 – PART 1

765.   Exhaustion
766.   A Wendy House
767.   Gone Poachin'
768.   A Rolls Royce
769.   'Market'
770.   His pension
771.   The Boer War

772. In the garden shed
773. £25
774. Out of Order

SERIES 4 – PART 1
775. Champ
776. Two
777. Woolly hats and thermal underwear
778. A chimpanzee
779. Bassett
780. Mars Bar
781. Working on an oil rig
782. Del reckoned the drivers would be cleaning out the cars
783. A summons
784. A leg of pork

TRIGGER
785. Dave
786. He said Del Boy was giving him a lift to the pub
787. Road sweeper
788. False
789. He was her uncle
790. He said they could hitchhike
791. Stockholm (*Sweden*)
792. His eye
793. Birth certificate and passport
794. A Jelly

SERIES 5 – PART 1
795. HM Customs & Excise (VAT people)
796. (i) Medals (ii) O.B.E. (iii) Nobel Peace Prize
797. (i) Shelf Packers (ii) Porters (iii) Cleaners (iv) Security

798. Ford Sierra

799. *Jaws*

800. Australia

801. His degree

802. Radio Rentals

803. Shoe size

804. A calculator

MIXED BAG 11

805. Laker (*Freddie Laker*)

806. Everything in the flat

807. A dinner service and two Persian rugs

808. The Master Bedroom

809. Volvo

810. Asthma

811. 15

812. Saint George

813. Del Boy had it in his hands and as Denzil approached,
      Del Boy told him that he had his money for him. Thinking
      that Del's hands were outstretched to greet him, Denzil
      slapped them, killing the butterfly instantly.

814. A petition

'WHO WANTS TO BE A MILLIONAIRE?'

815. Jumbo Mills

816. A music licence

817. Fog

818. A fish stall

819. Del Boy bet Boycie that Jumbo was wearing a wig

820. £10

821. Rolls-Royce and Mercedes

822. Prince Charles

823. Del Boy would be responsible for sales
824. He had a criminal record

'A ROYAL FLUSH'

825. Canteens of cutlery
826. Indonesia
827. Third Party, Fire and Theft
828. Victoria
829. Her Paintings
830. A partnership!
831. The Art Gallery (The National Gallery)
832. The opera
833. Sleep
834. A tourist

'THE FROG'S LEGACY'

835. A computer
836. £399
837. The River Nile
838. Trigger claimed that he had also received a few certificates after drinking it (*sick lines*)
839. His suitcase
840. Funeral Director
841. Lisa
842. Del thought Rodney would be getting a Citroen car (*CV model*)
843. A dinner set
844. The bomb squad

'DATES'

845. Ladies electric razor
846. Uncle Albert's
847. Letters and photographs from his days in the Navy

848.   17
849.   Ray Charles
850.   Trigger
851.   The Masons
852.   Bus Inspector
853.   Steak
854.   Racquel

'YUPPY LOVE'

855.   A Diploma in Computing
856.   That the flat was 15 minutes from the ground
857.   North Sea
858.   Porsche
859.   The Commodities Market
860.   A Beaujolais Nouveau
861.   Rodney had lifted her raincoat by mistake
862.   Trigger
863.   A pork pie
864.   Wet Wet Wet

'DANGER UXD'

865.   Del Boy said they would send it a postcard
866.   Tomatoes
867.   Boeuf Bourguignon
868.   Express
869.   They wanted to get away from Del Boy who had
       been hanging around the wine bars
870.   Perrier
871.   A slice of bread
872.   An explosive gas
873.   The boys dressed them up in their mum's clothes
874.   He said he wasn't insured

 **ANSWERS**

'CHAIN GANG'

875. The '*One Eleven Club*'
876. A windsock
877. Arnie
878. A Jaguar
879. 250
880. Boycie, Mike, Rodney, Trigger and Uncle Albert
881. Italian
882. An ambulance
883. The Highcliffe Hotel, Guernsey
884. Denzil

SERIES 3 – PART 2

885. A cigarette case
886. An Iranian
887. The Water Works
888. A painting (*his Gran's painting that had been hanging in the flat*)
889. Immunity from prosecution
890. A saucer of milk
891. Strawberries
892. Three
893. Mrs Mop
894. Gas fire

SERIES 4 – PART 2

895. The Job Centre
896. Germany
897. Lampposts
898. A Stetson (*White*)
899. Wardrobes in the houses that were being built on a new housing estate
900. He stole some watches

901. Luxury Flats and a Marina
902. He said that Uncle Albert kept forgetting that he could not walk
903. Bo Derek (*from the Movie, '10'*)
904. A lily pad

SERIES 5 – PART 2
905. His leg
906. Taiwan
907. The Metropolitan Water Board
908. A social worker
909. A syrup
910. Mickey said she had just come off duty
911. (i) A solarium (ii) A swimming pool
912. A telephone (*plug-in*)
913. *Ben-Hur*
914. His mouth

MIXED BAG – 12
915. The local building site
916. Del Boy asked her to
917. Del Boy telephoned him and pretended to be the local area health inspector
918. Champagne
919. A solid gold watch
920. Close his head in the door
921. The fishmongers
922. Uncle Albert's cap (*Del threw it at the butterfly as it was sitting on a grave*)
923. Smile
924. Charlton Heston

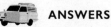 **ANSWERS**

'THE UNLUCKY WINNER IS…'

925. Dawn
926. L'Arc de Triomphe
927. Birdseye
928. Which Car?
929. Mega Flakes
930. Mallorca
931. Comb, tub of Vicks and a film for a camera
932. The Groovy Gang
933. Spanish Lottery tickets
934. Break dancing

'SICKNESS AND WEALTH'

935. A Dalek
936. Chinese
937. Robbie Meadows
938. Brandy
939. A Medium (*Spiritualist*)
940. He organised a séance
941. Her wooden leg
942. Nerys (*Nervous Nerys*)
943. New Delhi
944. Stress

'LITTLE PROBLEMS'

945. He failed his computer exam
946. Cassandra's father at his print factory
947. Mobile Phones
948. D.I.C.
949. Horseracing
950. Jevon and Mickey Pearce
951. The Driscoll Brothers

952. The Boer War
953. Holding Back The Years
954. He returned to Del Boy's flat instead of his own by mistake

SERIES 6 – PART 1
955. Del Boy claimed that breakfast was for wimps
956. Her wig
957. A mantelpiece
958. Knocking the paint off them
959. The Register
960. A 'connery' (*a heart attack*)
961. Cynthia (Cynthia Paine)
962. Mercedes-Benz
963. The Green Cross Code Man
964. Junior disco

'THE JOLLY BOYS' OUTING'
965. Car radio/cassette players
966. Margate
967. The computer department
968. Africa
969. *Fabrique Belgique*
970. Baseball
971. Trivial Pursuit
972. Beano (*going on a beano to Margate*)
973. Denzil, Jevon, Mickey and Rodney
974. The Villa Bella

'RODNEY COME HOME'
975. A couple of hamburgers
976. Racquel
977. '*Man Overboard*', '*Ship Ahoy*' & '*There She Blows*'

978. A Vow of Loudness
979. '*The Dark*'
980. He was eating a sandwich from his waste paper basket
981. Badminton
982. Del Boy singed it when he lit the candles
983. A Darts Team
984. '*Dodgy*'

'THE SKY'S THE LIMIT'

985. In Rodney's old room
986. Half a Grapefruit
987. *The Financial Times* and *Exchange & Mart*
988. A Lada
989. Viral Condition (*Sore stomach*)
990. J. Edgar (*J. Edgar Hoover*)
991. Manchester
992. Bronco
993. Stars
994. Gatwick

'THE CHANCE OF A LUNCHTIME'

995. Jam biscuits
996. His cigar went into it
997. Rehearse her new play
998. Musical doorbells that played national anthems
999. Del Boy said he missed Rodney like George Michael missed Andrew Ridgley
1000. He left a note with each of them telling them that the other one wanted to meet them
1001. An ex-fiancée
1002. Jules
1003. He resigned from his position at the Print Factory

1004.　Racquel was pregnant

'STAGE FRIGHT'

1005.　His own parking space

1006.　His '*little embryo*'

1007.　Companies House

1008.　False tan, gold rings, dark sunglasses, a salami and a wig

1009.　'R'

1010.　The Trotter International Star Agency

1011.　The nearest door

1012.　'Crying' by Roy Orbison

1013.　Bus fare (*Uncle Albert had a bus pass*)

1014.　'*Stick with me son and I will make you wich*'

'THE CLASS OF '62'

1015.　The Nag's Head

1016.　Roy Slater

1017.　Fax machine (*with a built-in copier*)

1018.　Boycie, Denzil, Rodney, Uncle Albert and Trigger

1019.　Bamber Gascoigne (*University Challenege*)

1020.　Camaraderie

1021.　Rachel

1022.　John Barnes

1023.　Champagne

1024.　Diamonds

'HE AIN'T HEAVY, HE'S MY UNCLE'

1025.　Gazza (*Paul Gascoigne*)

1026.　*A Nightmare On Elm Street*

1027.　Dominoes

1028.　That he had been mugged

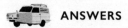

1029. *Out of Africa*
1030. He wet himself
1031. A Ford Capri Ghia
1032. Tobacco
1033. Policemen
1034. Boxing

'THREE MEN, A WOMAN AND A BABY'

1035. A curry
1036. Rodney
1037. Hair pieces – clip-on pony tails, wigs etc
1038. Mickey Pearce
1039. Sting
1040. Nelson Mandela
1041. His wig fell off
1042. Numbers on the baby's head
1043. Damien
1044. He said that this time next year they would be millionaires

SERIES 7 – PART 1

1045. A policeman
1046. Trudy
1047. Another load of Indians
1048. Shirley Bassey
1049. The Prat Mobile
1050. Tokyo
1051. '*Bellyache*' & '*Egg-bound*'
1052. France
1053. Trigger
1054. Mike

SERIES 6 – PART 2

1055. Jersey

1056. The 1812 Overture

1057. So as his entry would be on top of the pile of other entries

1058. It was clamped

1059. R2D2

1060. He did not allocate it a sufficient amount of fuel

1061. The barman lifted part of the bar counter and as Del Boy casually lent back to lean on it, he fell

1062. Del Boy sold him the Plaque

1063. The VAT

1064. Her bikini line

MIXED BAG – 13

1065. The snooker hall

1066. His living room

1067. 10

1068. Muggers

1069. Jonah

1070. Del asked Uncle Albert if she had been caught with her finger in a till

1071. Nettles (*stingy nettles*)

1072. They followed the Hull–Zeebrugge Ferry

1073. Kuala Lumpur

1074. Prawn Balls

'MIAMI TWICE: THE AMERICAN DREAM' – 1

1075. For Damien's christening

1076. On the roof of Del Boy's Ford Capri Ghia

1077. Pre-blessed Communion Wine

1078. Boycie, Marlene and Tyler

1079. As his Maxwell money

1080. She had to attend a seminar organised by the bank
1081. She switched the baby intercom on in the bedroom
1082. Because the ticket was in the name of 'Trotter'
       and not transferable
1083. A nappy
1084. Richard Branson

'MIAMI TWICE: THE AMERICAN DREAM' – 2

1085. Damien Derek Trotter
1086. The Book of Prophets (*pronounced 'Profits' by Del Boy*)
1087. Romania
1088. Lourdes
1089. The Omen
1090. Marlene (*Boycie's wife*)
1091. Fergie
1092. Del Boy's and Racquel's bedroom
1093. Leopard Skin
1094. Biggles

'MIAMI TWICE: OH TO BE IN ENGLAND' – 1

1095. Virgin Atlantic
1096. A Camper Van
1097. Del Boy said he promised to telephone Racquel
       as soon as they arrived
1098. Occhetti
1099. Australian
1100. Barry Gibb
1101. Columbia
1102. A Tropical Storm had cut all the phone lines off
1103. Ascot (*she said she had been to Royal Ascot*)
1104. It was in the shape of a Globe

'MIAMI TWICE: OH TO BE IN ENGLAND' – 2

1105. The Glitterati
1106. A bra
1107. He ran off with Del Boy's camera
1108. A curry
1109. *The Yellow Rose of Texas*
1110. He told the Don that he could not prove his innocence because he was guilty
1111. Del Boy put it in his mouth and sucked it
1112. Lurch
1113. Noofter
1114. Puskas

'MOTHER NATURE'S SON' – 1

1115. Merry Xmas Everybody
1116. Gums
1117. Myles
1118. A sterilised baby bottle
1119. Denzil and Trigger
1120. 'Peckham Spring'
1121. Cassandra (*she was in charge of the Bank's 'Small Business Investment' Department*)
1122. Brighton
1123. The Grand
1124. It began to glow

'MOTHER NATURE'S SON' – 2

1125. Ken Dodd
1126. A deep sea diver's suit
1127. The flat
1128. French beans
1129. A prison sentence

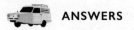

1130. Alan Titmarsh
1131. Some more delivery vans
1132. The Presidential Suite
1133. 'Earhole'
1134. It ran out of water

'FATAL EXTRACTION' – 1
1135. Rioting
1136. His pants and vests
1137. His tooth
1138. Video cameras
1139. His highchair
1140. A gerbil
1141. The dentists
1142. Trigger
1143. An answering machine
1144. Silent Night

'FATAL EXTRACTION' – 2
1145. Beans, Eggs and Sausages
1146. On the bus
1147. Skiing clothes and equipment
1148. At Cassandra and Rodney's flat
1149. Lime
1150. Hobnobs
1151. A bottle of champagne
1152. Sing
1153. Psychiatric Hospital
1154. A china ornament

FEATURE LENGTH SPECIALS – 1

1155. A Boomtown Rat
1156. Ladies Electric Razors
1157. Egypt
1158. Hannibal Lecter
1159. Two glass cuff-link inserts
1160. The Duke of Mowbray
1161. (i) Accessory to three counts of murder (ii) Drug smuggling
     (iii) Kidnapping
1162. A computer
1163. He threw it over the balcony at the flat
1164. Piranha

MIXED BAG – 14

1165. Johnny & Ron
1166. A convertible
1167. Royal Doulton
1168. A snake
1169. Gold Teeth
1170. A French stick of bread
1171. A Spaceman
1172. (i) Import Licences (ii) Customs Clearance (iii) Re-Registration
     & (iv) New Log Books
1173. Frog's Spawn
1174. James Bond

SERIES 7 – PART 2

1175. Gerald Ford (*Betty Ford was mentioned*)
1176. 18
1177. Boycie and Mike
1178. 'Reject'
1179. Nuts

1180. Name Del Boy and Racquel's baby
1181. His next-door neighbour – a Chief Inspector
1182. Low Demand Accommodation
1183. Her tan
1184. Green (*Lime Green*)

'HEROES AND VILLAINS' – 1

1185. Trotter Air, Trotters Meat Fingers and Trotterex
    (*a condom-type product*)
1186. A football
1187. Uncle Albert drank it
1188. The RAC
1189. Batman (*Del Boy*) and Robin (*Rodney*)
1190. He held his suitcase at head height and the mugger ran into it
1191. Linford Christie
1192. Rooney
1193. Cassandra was expecting a baby
1194. A home improvement grant

'HEROES AND VILLAINS' – 2

1195. Lord Trotter of Peckham
1196. A rabbit
1197. Radio alarm clocks
1198. A chunky gold ID bracelet
1199. For saving the Council money – he claimed to have had the
    same broom for 20 years
1200. He ignited his cigarette lighter so as he could see in the dark
1201. The Joker
1202. Trigger
1203. Baseball caps
1204. A medal

'MODERN MEN' – 1

1205. Epping Forest
1206. Modern men
1207. Fur (*Simulated Fur*)
1208. Vasectomy
1209. His job
1210. Nat West
1211. Dr Singh
1212. Motorbike crash helmets
1213. He burst out crying
1214. He hit him a dig on the chin

'MODERN MEN' – 2

1215. Nuts
1216. Green
1217. St Valentine's Day
1218. Penetration
1219. Uncle Albert claimed that Rodney could not get them to work
1220. 'Old Shep'
1221. Tadpoles
1222. One of Racquel's old scarves
1223. Sales
1224. Mike

FEATURE LENGTH SPECIALS – 2

1225. Russia
1226. Mad Cow Disease
1227. British Airways
1228. Cilla Black
1229. Japan
1230. Bucharest
1231. Three lions on a shirt

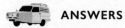

1232. What is a female swan called?
1233. Barry Sheene
1234. He was on a jet ski that had its steering mechanism locked

'TIME ON OUR HANDS' – 1

1235. A recipe book
1236. The Russian convoys
1237. He used coffee granules by mistake
1238. Michael Aspel
1239. WD40
1240. Trotter Manor
1241. A motor launch
1242. All three of them ended up paying a visit to the flat
1243. Carpet steamers
1244. The Futures Market

'TIME ON OUR HANDS' – 2

1245. Lamb
1246. Acne
1247. James
1248. Skoda
1249. Ghandi
1250. Sotheby's
1251. £6.2 million
1252. Snooker
1253. The 11-Plus
1254. Billionaires

'IF THEY COULD SEE US NOW' – 1

1255. The British Museum
1256. The Queen (*Del Boy*) and The Duke of Edinburgh (*Rodney*)
1257. Hotel de Paris and Dominic

1258. Elsie Partridge
1259. 'Livin' La Vida Loca'
1260. Russel Crowe – a Roman Centurion or Gladiator
1261. Goldrush
1262. Penalty
1263. Damien
1264. Give it to Charity

'IF THEY COULD SEE US NOW' – 2

1265. 'A Touch of Glass', 'Danger UXD', 'Heroes and Villains' and 'The Jolly Boys' Outing'
1266. They turned up at the wrong funeral
1267. Bankruptcy court (*London*)
1268. Boycie, Denzil, Sid and Trigger
1269. Brunei
1270. 'Can't Get You Out Of My Head'
1271. A Policewoman
1272. £1 minimum and £100,000 maximum
1273. Jonathan Ross
1274. Shoes

'STRANGERS ON THE SHORE' – 1

1275. Cleaning Boycie's car
1276. *The Beano*
1277. Bob Marley
1278. Log effect
1279. Onion purée
1280. A Hoover bag
1281. The American (*USA*)
1282. An illegal immigrant
1283. Gary
1284. The Gary Gang

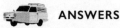

'STRANGERS ON THE SHORE' – 2

1285. Mini
1286. Monkey Harris
1287. A dart
1288. A Vasectomy
1289. Denzil
1290. A beret
1291. Del Boy
1292. Champs d Elysses
1293. Del Boy's pyjamas (*lime green*) and his dressing gown (*red*)
1294. Boycie

'SLEEPLESS IN PECKHAM' – 1

1295. $ (dollar symbol)
1296. Mobile phone, sunglasses and walkman
1297. Denzil
1298. The Official Receiver
1299. The screenplay for a movie
1300. Carlsberg (*Special Brew*) and Tennents
1301. Freddie The Frog (*Frederick Robdul*)
1302. To hear the reading of their Uncle Albert's Last Will & Testament
1303. Art
1304. Joan

'SLEEPLESS IN PECKHAM' – 2

1305. Bacon and Rolos
1306. A goalkeeper
1307. A fold-away backscratcher
1308. Mel Gibson
1309. Trotter
1310. She was recovering after having breast implants
1311. '*Sing*'

1312. Trigger
1313. Solitary confinement
1314. Cartwright

MIXED BAG – 15

1315. Rolls-Royce
1316. Tonic and Lime
1317. In the hood of Uncle Albert's Duffle Coat
1318. Denzil's brothers
1319. Getting engaged
1320. Security
1321. He said he was afraid that she may not be as sick
       as people said she was
1322. The Town Hall
1323. Persian
1324. Berkshire

EXPERT: DEL BOY

1325. Edward
1326. As their 'Boardroom and Factory Floor'
1327. Captured German machine gun nests
1328. 'Tres Bien Ensemble'
1329. Oklahoma
1330. Barratts
1331. Sinbad
1332. 'Cats, Cats, Miaow, Miaow'
1333. Nelson
1334. Figaro from *The Barber of Seville*

EXPERT: RODNEY

1335. Linda
1336. £4.37

1337. Zowie
1338. Charlton
1339. Peking
1340. Bernice
1341. Boney Ms
1342. Playboy
1343. Basingstoke
1344. Meryl Streep

EXPERT: SERIES 1
1345. Bobby Finch
1346. The Tyler Street Bus & Coach Garage
1347. A hamburger
1348. George
1349. 'Sean'
1350. No Waiting
1351. OLD 190P
1352. 'Afternoon'
1353. A Rolls-Royce Cornish
1354. USA & Tim

EXPERT: SERIES 2
1355. She was on Riot Patrol
1356. 'Zoom' – by Fat Larry's Band
1357. Alice
1358. Yves Saint Dior
1359. GBH, Wounding With Intent and Attempted Murder
1360. Del Boy – 'Away Day Gold' and Rodney – 'Inter-City Yellow'
1361. Genuine Italian sun hats
1362. 'Doctor's orders'
1363. The Magaluf Brothers
1364. Bo Derek

EXPERT: SERIES 3

1365. The Star Of Bengal
1366. The Flying Squad and SGB
1367. Tyres
1368. For not having a tax disc on the van
1369. The Chinese Detective
1370. Cheery Blossom Poisoning (referring to how much we was licking his boss's shoes)
1371. *Johnny Cash, Live at San Quentin*
1372. Coventry Street
1373. Rhanji
1374. Tenerife

EXPERT: SERIES 4

1375. Sheena Easton
1376. The roof of a building at the cemetery
1377. Silk Cut
1378. A bus [ass
1379. 'What's Up Doc?', 'Exterminate' & 'Boo Boo'
1380. 24
1381. Pedigree Chum
1382. Paddy The Greek (*Del actually sold them to Paddy The Greek the previous week*)
1383. 166
1384. Deirdre

EXPERT: SERIES 5

1385. Louis Armstrong
1386. Rumpelstiltskin
1387. The One-Eleven (111) Club
1388. 'The Rose Of Peckham' (*he had previously told Rodney he named her 'Miss 999'*)

 **ANSWERS**

1389. '*There is a rhinoceros loose in the city*'
1390. Dillingers 75
1391. (i) Perjury (ii) Embezzlement (iii) Conspiring to pervert
the course of justice (iv) Fraudulent conversion of travellers cheques
1392. A marble tiled gazebo
1393. 'How?' (in reference to how red Rodney's face was)
1394. *Emmanuel* in Peckham

EXPERT: SERIES 6
1395. A boil
1396. Peckham Courier Service
1397. Del Boy blew cigar smoke into the car and she almost
choked coughing
1398. Knitting
1399. An onion bhaji
1400. Samaritans
1401. The Kings Avenue
1402. Folkestone
1403. Mineral water
1404. Spanish law prohibited gambling by under-18s

EXPERT: SERIES 7
1405. She noticed some egg yolk on his chin
1406. *As You Like It*
1407. A Pot Noodle
1408. Parkhurst
1409. On safari
1410. Mickey Pearce
1411. Chernobyl
1412. His ears
1413. Eric
1414. Agatha Christie

EXPERT: FEATURE LENGTH SPECIALS - 1

1415. The radio/cassette player being on fire
1416. A Big Mac
1417. Universe
1418. Davy Smith's
1419. Julia Roberts
1420. Look out for tulips and listen out or clogs
1421. Tom Jones
1422. Double glazing salesman
1423. Maxwell House
1424. Chris Boardman

EXPERT: FEATURE LENGTH SPECIALS – 2

1425. The kiss of life
1426. A glass of wine
1427. He said his father said he didn't know but that he tried
       to get a week off work with it
1428. Bulldog
1429. Special Branch
1430. Light wwitches
1431. A lighthouse rat
1432. The Aegean Sea
1433. His old headmistress
1434. The bishops

EXPERT: FEATURE LENGTH SPECIALS – 3

1435. £250
1436. Bunny Shadows
1437. Douche
1438. A Ferrari
1439. Christopher Columbus (*Del Boy called him 'Columbo'*)
1440. The Lone Ranger (*Rodney*) and Tonto (*Del Boy*)

1441. Towser
1442. David Bowie (*Ziggy Sawdust*) and Lordy Geordie
(*Robson & Jerome*)
1443. Four
1444. He was a frogman in the Royal Navy

EXPERT: 'A ROYAL FLUSH'

1445. The Hilton
1446. Carmen
1447. Swiss finishing school
1448. 12
1449. Arch Duke Ferdinand
1450. Del Boy said he liked birds and curry
1451. Handsome Samson
1452. Iggy Higgins
1453. Covington House
1454. 'Tommy'

EXPERT: 'CHAIN GANG'

1455. Otto
1456. Grayson
1457. Guernsey
1458. £200
1459. Maxi Stavros
1460. Pat
1461. Chelsea
1462. Mario
1463. St Stephens
1464. Gary and Steven

EXPERT: FEATURE LENGTH SPECIALS - 1

1415. The radio/cassette player being on fire
1416. A Big Mac
1417. Universe
1418. Davy Smith's
1419. Julia Roberts
1420. Look out for tulips and listen out or clogs
1421. Tom Jones
1422. Double glazing salesman
1423. Maxwell House
1424. Chris Boardman

EXPERT: FEATURE LENGTH SPECIALS – 2

1425. The kiss of life
1426. A glass of wine
1427. He said his father said he didn't know but that he tried to get a week off work with it
1428. Bulldog
1429. Special Branch
1430. Light wwitches
1431. A lighthouse rat
1432. The Aegean Sea
1433. His old headmistress
1434. The bishops

EXPERT: FEATURE LENGTH SPECIALS – 3

1435. £250
1436. Bunny Shadows
1437. Douche
1438. A Ferrari
1439. Christopher Columbus (*Del Boy called him 'Columbo'*)
1440. The Lone Ranger (*Rodney*) and Tonto (*Del Boy*)

ANSWERS

1441. Towser
1442. David Bowie (*Ziggy Sawdust*) and Lordy Geordie
(*Robson & Jerome*)
1443. Four
1444. He was a frogman in the Royal Navy

EXPERT: 'A ROYAL FLUSH'

1445. The Hilton
1446. Carmen
1447. Swiss finishing school
1448. 12
1449. Arch Duke Ferdinand
1450. Del Boy said he liked birds and curry
1451. Handsome Samson
1452. Iggy Higgins
1453. Covington House
1454. 'Tommy'

EXPERT: 'CHAIN GANG'

1455. Otto
1456. Grayson
1457. Guernsey
1458. £200
1459. Maxi Stavros
1460. Pat
1461. Chelsea
1462. Mario
1463. St Stephens
1464. Gary and Steven

EXPERT: 'DATES'

1465. Taiwan

1466. HMS *Peerless*

1467. USS *Pittsburgh*

1468. Comic Relief Day

1469. '*The Technomatch Computer Dating Agency*' but also referred to in the show as 'The Technomatch Friendship and Matrimonial Agency'

1470. Hilton Hotel, London

1471. Zephyr

1472. A Lizard Person

1473. Double cream

1474. An angler's knife (made of Sheffield Steel)

EXPERT: 'DANGER UXD'

1475. Matzuki

1476. City News

1477. £2.75

1478. Chloe and Adrian

1479. Clayton Cooper

1480. £30 each

1481. Playthings

1482. Dusseldorf

1483. They were lying beside the hot-air duct and Rodney thought the heat in the flat had set off the canisters of gas inside the dolls

1484. Erotic Estelle and Lusty Linda

EXPERT: MIXED BAG – 1

1485. 'Chow Min' (*close to 'Chow Mein'*)

1486. 25 pence

1487. Jackie

1488. Brian
1489. Fatty Walker
1490. A bad day at Blue Cross
1491. £45
1492. He was a porter
1493. Albert Gladstone Trotter
1494. No. 26

EXPERT: MIXED BAG – 2

1495. Connie
1496. 'Tiny Jack Boots'
1497. Rosanna
1498. She came up to London to purchase a wedding dress
1499. Chas
1500. Pink
1501. Green – Grandad, Purple – Rodney
1502. Gillian
1503. Peabody Buildings, Peckham Rye
1504. Anarkali